For Rosemary, to help
you cook genuine
Southern style!

Kathryn T. Windham

November 20, 1980

Every man should eat and drink, and enjoy the good of all his labour, it is the gift of God.

ECCLESIASTES 3:13.

Southern Cooking To Remember

by
Kathryn Tucker Windham

Illustrated
by

Marjorie M. Stewart

THE STRODE PUBLISHERS, INC.
HUNTSVILLE, ALABAMA 35802

CONTENTS

PREFACE

Commercialized "Southern cooking," the kind advertised by gaudy signs along thousands of highways in the Deep South, has almost spoiled the reputation of real Southern food.

Real Southern food, despite what its crass promoters and its bigoted detractors say, is not always fried, nor is it typically greasy or heavy or monotonous. And the notion that it must have its taste disguised by heavy slatherings of catsup is blasphemous.

Southern food is as delightful and as varied and as interesting as the region from which it comes: shrimp gumbo simmered along the Gulf Coast, roast venison from Alabama's piney woods, wild ducks from Georgia's marshlands, tall stacks of Tennessee mountain in-fare cakes, charlotte piled high in crystal bowls, dewberry cobbler, scuppernong wine, tender turnip greens with wedges of hot corn-bread, peas cooked with ham hocks, Brunswick stew made by an old family recipe, fresh fish and hush puppies, chess pie, squash souffle, spoon bread, smothered quail with baked grits, chicken fried to a crisp (ungreasy) brown, thick slices of country ham with red-eye gravy—the list goes on and on as good Deep South cooks and dis-criminating diners add their all-time favorite foods.

Here is a collection of real Deep South recipes, a sampling of the foods that make even the simplest Southern meal a memorable experience.

Beverages

BEVERAGES

Pink lemonade
Made in the shade
And stirred
With a spade.

On summer Sunday afternoons, back before air conditioning imprisoned families inside their homes, drinking tall glasses of lemonade on the front porch (or on the back porch if the front porch was too sunny) was a family ritual across the South. Truth is lots more Southerners drank lemonade than ever tasted mint juleps.

First on those Sundays came Sunday School and worship services. Families gathered in frame churches, their windows open wide as a petition for relief from the heavy heat, to sing and to pray and to listen to the Word.

After church, after a brief time of complaining about the weather and exchanging news with friends, came Sunday dinner, a big meal with fresh vegetables, rice and gravy, hot biscuits and corn bread, fried chicken or roast beef, cake or pie, and iced tea ("Don't use all the ice—save some for the lemonade!").

Then everybody took a nap. Or nearly everybody did. Those who did not go to sleep had to keep quiet: no door slamming, no radio playing, no loud talking, no skating on the porch. Sunday silence enveloped the house.

The lengths of those naps varied. Some afternoons it was too hot to sleep. Sometimes the persistence of mosquitoes, disturbances in the chicken yard, the buzzing of a pesky fly, or the barking of a dog would arouse the sleepers.

Always the official signal that naptime had ended was the creaking of the roller at the well: somebody was getting ready to make lemonade. For lemonade was always made with water freshly drawn from the back-porch well. Even after indoor plumbing was installed, water from the well, pulled up hand over hand to the accompaniment of the creaking roller, continued to be used for iced tea, for lemonade, and for just plain drinking.

Meantime in the kitchen, the lemons were brought in from the glass bowl on the sideboard in the dining room, were cut on the metal-covered counter, and squeezed on a heavy glass reamer. The seeds were carefully removed from the rim, where they floated like elusive fish in a lemony moat.

Some families made lemonade by the pitchersful. Others made it by the glassful, fixing each glass to suit the individual taste of each family member ("Be sure to put extra sugar in Aunt Bet's glass....Just a little more lemon juice in Daddy's....").

Then, last of all, the ice was cracked to cool the waiting glasses. The ice pick was pulled from the wall where the last user had thrust it, and hunks of ice were chipped from the dwindling block ("It's a good thing the iceman will come in the morning!") in the wooden icebox.

Out on the front porch, the gathered family moved the rocking chairs around to catch a breeze, to avoid the glare from the sun. And somebody cleared off the green table in the corner, pushed aside the tall vase of crepe myrtle blossoms and the accumulation of newspapers and Sunday School quarterlies, to make room for the tray with its cool glasses of lemonade.

Summer Sunday afternoons—and lemonade.

PARSON'S PUNCH

2 cups grape juice
1 cup pineapple juice
1 cup water

1/3 cup lemon juice
Sugar to taste
Crushed ice

Put ripe grapes in cheesecloth bag and squeeze out the juice. Add the juice to other ingredients, stirring in enough sugar to suit the tastes of the drinkers. If wild grapes are not available, bottled grape juice may be substituted.

SUMMER AFTERNOON PUNCH

1 pint strong tea
3 cups orange juice
2/3 cup lemon juice

1 cup pineapple juice
2/3 cup sugar
1 large bottle ginger ale

Mix all ingredients except ginger ale and chill well. At serving time, add ginger ale. Serve over cracked ice, garnishing each serving with orange wedges, pineapple chunks, or strawberries, if desired.

WHITE RIBBON PARTY PUNCH

2 quarts ginger ale
2 quarts lemonade
1 6-ounce can frozen
   orange juice

1 quart pink lemonade
1 cup syrup from canned
   fruit cocktail

Chill all ingredients and combine in large punch bowl. Add sugar, if needed, to taste.

HEIRLOOM BLACKBERRY WINE

Wash blackberries well. Pour off water. Some will stick to the berries, but that is all right. Crush berries with hands (the juice will stain, so you may want to wear rubber gloves) and strain through a double thickness of cheesecloth, pressing cloth to get out all the juice. Measure juice and add sugar in the proportion of three pounds of sugar to each gallon of juice. Stir well. Let 'stand several hours to make sure sugar is dissolved, stirring every time you pass by. Pour into wide-mouthed jars (fruit jars). Fill each jar to the top and cover each with a piece of cheesecloth. Save one jar of juice to be used in refilling — those instructions are coming! Next morning skim off all the substance that has risen to the tops of the jars. Then refill the jars to the tops again, using the juice from the jar reserved for that purpose. Repeat this process for nine mornings. By that time the juice should be clear and the fermentation should have stopped. Then slowly and carefully pour wine from jars into bottles. Do not disturb — or attempt to save — dregs in bottoms of jars. Cover tops of bottles with cheesecloth for two or three days until wine has stopped "working" so bottles won't explode. Then cork tightly and store in a cool place. Age does fine things to this wine.

SCUPPERNONG WINE

1 quart (heaping) scuppernongs   **½ cup warm water**
  or muscadines   **6 cups sugar**
1 envelope dry yeast

Pop hulls of grapes, saving hulls, pulp, and juice. Dissolve yeast in ½ cup warm water. Place yeast in bottom of gallon crock, add ¾ cup water, and stir. Put sugar into crock and add enough water to fill about half full. Stir well. Add grapes (hulls, pulp, and juice), leaving about four or five inches of space at the top of container. Cover (tie) with cheesecloth or dish towel and let set for three weeks. Lift fruit out and let wine stand in crock another week. Strain and bottle.

FESTIVE CHAMPAGNE PUNCH

2 large bottles champagne
1 large bottle white wine
1 cup brandy

1 quart sparkling water
1 cup syrup drained from canned
   fruit cocktail

Chill all ingredients and combine in punch bowl. Add Champagne Ring (recipe follows) to float in punch and serve to about twenty guests.

Champagne Ring

Mint leaves
1 large can (29 ounces)
   fruit cocktail, drained

6 ounces pink
   lemonade concentrate
1 quart champagne

Place mint leaves and some fruit cocktail in bottom of ring mold. Mix pink lemonade concentrate (do not dilute) with champagne and put just enough of this mixture in ring mold to cover mint leaves and hold fruit in place. Freeze. When leaves and fruit are frozen in place, add remaining liquid and fruit. Return to freezer until very firm. Unmold and float pretty side up in punch.

For a non-alcoholic fruit ring, substitute ginger ale for champagne.

PUNCH FOR THIRSTY CROWD (ADULT)

3 6-ounce cans frozen
   orange juice
1 6-ounce can frozen
   lemon juice
1 6-ounce can frozen
   lime juice

1 No. 2 can pineapple juice
2 quarts water
1 quart ginger ale
1 pint vodka
2 limes, sliced
1 lemon, sliced

Mix fruit juices and water and chill. Just before serving, add ginger ale and vodka and pour over block of ice in punch bowl. Add slices of lemon and lime. A few drops of red or green food coloring may be added if desired.

SPECIAL OCCASION EGGNOG

2 cups whipping cream
1 cup sugar
1 dozen eggs, separated

1½ cups fine bourbon
Sprinkling of nutmeg

This eggnog is best prepared by hand without the assistance of electric mixers. Hand-turned rotary beaters or wire egg whisks work fine. Whip cream until stiff and then slowly fold ¼ cup sugar into it. Beat egg yolks until light colored, and then slowly add bourbon, stirring gently to prevent curdling. Beat egg whites stiff and fold in ¾ cup sugar. Fold egg whites into yolk mixture. Handle gently—no beating. Fold in whipped cream, also gently. Serve in tall silver goblets with long silver spoons. Sprinkle each serving with nutmeg.

SPICED TEA MIX

1 cup instant tea (plain)
1 package lemonade mix
2 cups orange-flavored
    breakfast drink mix

2¾ cups sugar
1 teaspoon cloves
1½ teaspoons cinnamon

Combine all ingredients, mix well, and store in air-tight container. When ready to serve, mix three heaping teaspoons in a cup of boiling water, adjusting the amount to suit individual taste.

FUDDLED PEACHES

Peel and slice enough ripe peaches to fill a half-gallon jar. Put a layer of peaches on the bottom of the jar, cover with a layer of sugar, add another layer of sliced peaches, cover with sugar, and continue until jar is full, ending with layer of sugar. Pour a bottle of wine (it need not be the finest vintage) into the jar. Then put the top on (be sure the metal does not touch the contents of the jar), and hide the jar in a cool place for at least six months. If the sugar has not dissolved by that time, put the top back on and wait a few more weeks. When the sugar has dissolved and the whole thing has a heady, wonderful aroma, drain off the liquid and share it with a few dear friends. The peaches may be served with roast duck, Cornish hens, or such. They are mighty good eaten right out of the jar.

PUNCH FOR A CROWD

2 cups boiling water
3 cups sugar
2 packages strawberry
   drink mix
1 large can pineapple juice

1 can frozen lemonade
3 quarts water
1 package frozen strawberry
   slices
2 large bottles ginger ale

Boil two cups water and dissolve sugar in it. Let cool. Mix all other ingredients except frozen strawberries and ginger ale. Chill. Add fruit and ginger ale just before serving. Pour over block of ice in punch bowl.

Breads

BREADS

Bread...strengtheneth man's heart.
—Psalms 104:15

"Take two and butter them while they're hot," is about as Southern an expression as there is. All Southerners immediately recognize these words as an invitation to take two biscuits, home-made and hot from the oven, and slather them with butter, real butter. Those two biscuits are intended to satisfy the diner until the next batch browns and is borne into the dining room to be passed around the table.

Hot breads—biscuits, corn bread, muffins, rolls—are the foundation of the traditionally fine Southern cooking. Many of the region's brag cooks began learning the art while perched on a high kitchen stool watching the best cook in the family make up a batch of biscuits. And always the watching child was treated by being allowed to make a tiny pan (usually the metal lid of a discarded Calumet Baking

Powder can) of thimble biscuits for her dolls' tea party.

Those doll-sized biscuits, cut with Grandmother's silver thimble, marked the debut of many a little girl into the grown-up world of cooking.

Biscuits with browned patties of homemade sausage (well seasoned) inside them were the staple of many a school lunch bucket. A sophisticated version of this long-time favorite is the dainty biscuit (always homemade) filled with thin slices of ham now served at elegant luncheons and bridal receptions.

Biscuits were a favorite after-school treat, too. Children coming home in the afternoon headed straight for the kitchen where, in the warming oven of the wood stove, waited biscuits left over from the family's noon dinner. A thumb (not always real clean) was jabbed ("jooged" was the descriptive word generally used) down into the side of the plump biscuit, and the depression was filled with thick syrup poured from the pitcher on the kitchen table. Three or four jooged biscuits would tide a growing child over until suppertime.

Leftover biscuits, when there were any, were made into dessert by crumbling the biscuits coarsely and mixing the crumbs with beaten eggs, rich milk, sugar, and a sprinkling of cinnamon. The mixture was placed in a buttered pan, dotted with dabs of butter, and baked until done. It was served hot, usually with more butter and sometimes with a lemon sauce.

Then there's corn bread in all its variations: hoe cake, corn pone, spoon bread, egg bread, johnny cake, hush puppies, dodgers, and local mixtures often nameless. Southern corn bread is—but that's another whole chapter!

THIMBLE BISCUITS

Many a little Southern girl got her first cooking experience by making thimble biscuits. The biscuits are made by rolling out mother's leftover biscuit dough and cutting it with a thimble, preferably a silver one. Place tiny biscuits on lightly buttered pan (tops of baking powder cans used to be popular for this) and bake until brown. The dough may be slightly tough and grey from much handling. Never mind. Eat!

BEATEN BISCUITS

Almost nobody makes beaten biscuits any more, but every now and then somebody wants to know how. So here is how:

8 cups sifted flour   **1 cup lard**
1 teaspoon salt   **2 cups milk**
1 teaspoon baking powder

Sift flour, salt, and baking powder together at least twice, preferably three times. Mix in lard (fingers work best for this) until mixture is mealy. Add milk to form stiff dough. Place dough on floured surface and beat with a wooden rolling pin or a wooden mallet. Keep folding the dough and beating it (the old rule is 200 times for home folks and 400 times for high company) until blisters appear on the dough. Roll out about 1/3 inch thick, cut with small biscuit cutter (dough can be rolled into small balls and flattened if no small cutter is available), and place on ungreased baking sheet. Prick the top of each biscuit two or three times, making a pattern, with the tines of a silver fork. Bake in hot oven (450 degrees) 15 to 20 minutes. It is a lot of work and it makes a lot of biscuits. They will keep several days in a tightly closed box.

20

BUTTERMILK BISCUITS

2 cups flour
¾ teaspoon soda
½ teaspoon salt

4 tablespoons shortening
¾ cup buttermilk

Sift dry ingredients together. Cut in shortening with a proper pastry blender or with two forks until mixture has the appearance but not the texture of small white gravel. Pour buttermilk in all at once. Mix gently. Transfer dough to floured surface and knead tenderly six or seven times. Roll with floured rolling pin to ½ inch thickness. Cut to desired size (big for hungry families, smaller for company, thimble-size for doll tea parties), place on lightly greased baking sheet, and bake at 450 degrees until brown.

HONEY BUNS

10 tablespoons sugar
2 egg yolks
1½ teaspoons salt
1/3 cup shortening
1 cup warm milk

2 packages dry yeast
½ cup warm water
4½ cups flour
Brown sugar and cinnamon

Combine sugar, egg yolks, and salt. Stir shortening into warm milk and add. Dissolve yeast in warm water and add to first mixture. Gradually add flour to make a stiff dough. Let rise in greased bowl (covered) until double in size. Roll out on floured surface. Sprinkle with brown sugar and cinnamon (a few dots of butter add flavor, and at this point what do a few more calories matter?) roll up, and slice about an inch or a little more thick. Put each slice in a muffin tin which has been buttered and has had brown sugar sprinkled on the bottom. Let rise about 45 minutes before baking in 350 degree oven for 20 to 30 minutes.

FLOATING CLOUD BISCUITS

2 cups flour
4 teaspoons baking powder
1 tablespoon sugar
½ teaspoon salt

½ cup shortening
2/3 cup milk
1 beaten egg

Sift dry ingredients together. Cut in shortening until mixture resembles coarse crumbs. Combine milk and egg and add. Stir with fork. Knead gently on floured surface, roll out ¾ inch thick, cut, and bake on ungreased baking sheet at 450 degrees about 12 minutes. Waste no time getting them to the folks at the dining table.

CREAMY DROP BISCUITS

2 cups sifted flour
1 teaspoon baking powder
1 teaspoon salt

2 beaten eggs
¾ cup heavy cream

Sift dry ingredients together and add eggs and cream. Stir just to mix—dough should be lumpy and soft. Use a tablespoon to drop hunks of dough onto greased baking sheet. Bake at 400 degrees about 15 minutes. This recipe makes a dozen big biscuits.

QUEEN OF MUFFINS

¼ cup butter—very soft
½ cup sugar
1 beaten egg
1½ cups flour

2½ teaspoons baking powder
½ teaspoon salt
2/3 cup milk

Cream butter and sugar. Add beaten egg. Sift dry ingredients together and add alternately with milk. Stir gently. Do not beat.

Bake in greased muffin rings at 400 degrees for about 20 minutes. This recipe may be varied by adding chopped dates, nuts, raisins, or even crumbled, crisp bacon to the batter.

PLEASE-PASS-THE-PUFFS

2 cups flour
1/3 cup sugar
3 teaspoons baking powder
1 teaspoon salt
1 teaspoon nutmeg
¾ cup milk

¼ cup salad oil
1 beaten egg
½ cup sugar
1 teaspoon cinnamon
Hot oil for deep frying

Sift first five ingredients together. Combine milk, oil, and beaten egg and add to first mixture, beating until smooth. Drop small portions into hot fat (375 degrees) about four inches deep. Fry a few at a time until golden brown. Drain. Roll in mixture of ½ cup sugar and 1 teaspoon cinnamon. Powdered sugar may be used instead of the granulated variety—cooks and eaters decide.

AUNT MAGRUDER'S PIGEON-TOED PINEAPPLE MUFFINS

2 cups sifted flour
¼ cup sugar
1 tablespoon baking powder
1 teaspoon salt
1 well-beaten egg

1 cup crushed pineapple
  (undrained)
2/3 cup milk
1½ teaspoons grated orange rind
2 tablespoons salad oil

Sift together flour, sugar, baking powder, and salt. Combine egg, crushed pineapple, milk, orange rind, and oil. Add gradually to dry ingredients, stirring only until dry ingredients are moistened. Fill greased muffin cups 2/3 full and bake at 425 degrees for 20 to 25 minutes.

ALMOST-INSTANT YEAST ROLLS

2 cups flour
1½ tablespoons sugar
1 teaspoon salt
1 teaspoon baking powder
1/3 cup shortening

1 package yeast
¼ cup warm water
¾ cup buttermilk
Melted butter
Sesame seeds (optional)

Sift dry ingredients together. Cut in shortening until grains are fairly fine. Dissolve yeast in warm water and add to buttermilk, stirring well. Pour this into dry ingredients and stir to mix thoroughly. Dump dough out on floured surface and knead, knead, knead (the recipe said "almost" instant!). Dough should be smooth and blistered. That is, the dough blistered—not hands. Now roll dough out about a quarter-inch thick and cut with biscuit cutter. Brush each circle with melted butter and fold over. Place on ungreased baking sheet, cover, and let rise for one hour. Bake at 400 degrees for about 13 minutes or until brown. During final stage of baking, brush tops with butter and sprinkle on sesame seeds, if desired.

FROSTED FRUIT BUNS

2 packages dry yeast
1¼ cups warm water
3½ cups sifted flour
2/3 teaspoon cinnamon
5½ tablespoons sugar
1 teaspoon salt

1 orange rind, shredded
¼ cup shortening
1 egg
½ cup seedless raisins
Frosting

Sprinkle yeast on water, let stand a few minutes, then stir until dissolved. Add half the flour, cinnamon, sugar, salt, shredded orange rind, shortening, and egg. Beat all these ingredients together until the mixture is smooth. Put in the rest of the flour and the raisins. Mix well. Cover (this generally means to cover with a fresh, clean dish towel) and let rise until double in bulk. This takes half an hour or so, depending on the temperature of the rising place. When doubled in bulk, stir the mixture down. Spoon it into greased muffin cups — two dozen of them — until the cups are half full. Let rise about 30 minutes. Bake at 425 degrees until brown and done, about 12 minutes. Cool. Cover tops with frosting made by mixing two cups confectioners' sugar with a dash of salt and about two tablespoons orange juice.

PLAYER PIANO GRAHAM GEMS

½ cup sifted flour

¼ cup sugar

1 teaspoon salt

4 teaspoons baking powder

1 cup whole wheat flour

1 beaten egg

1 cup milk

3 tablespoons butter or margarine, melted

Sift the first four ingredients into a big bowl, and then stir in the whole wheat flour. Beat the egg, milk, and butter together. Make a well in the middle of the dry ingredients (do this gently to avoid mashing the flour) and pour the liquid mixture into this depression. Stir only enough to moisten. Fill greased muffin pans about 2/3 full. Bake in hot (425 degree) oven about 15 minutes or until done. These graham gems became popular along about 1910 when the house with the player piano was the favorite gathering place.

QUICK BEER ROLLS

3 cups prepared biscuit mix

3 tablespoons sugar (scant)

Pinch salt

1 cup beer

Combine biscuit mix, sugar, and salt. Stir beer into batter. If it seems too stiff, add a little more beer. Drink what remains in can. Beat. Drop into greased muffin rings (it is the batter that is dropped) and bake at 375 degrees until brown.

RAISED MUFFINS

1 package yeast
¼ cup warm water
½ cup boiling water
¼ cup sugar
3 tablespoons butter or
   margarine

1½ teaspoons salt
½ cup evaporated milk,
   undiluted
2 beaten eggs
3½ cups sifted flour

Dissolve yeast in ¼ cup warm water. Pour boiling water over sugar, butter, and salt. Add milk, eggs, and dissolved yeast. Beat in about half the flour. Beat hard. Add remaining flour, beating vigorously. Cover and let rise until double. Beat again. Fill muffin cups 2/3 full. Let rise about an hour. Bake at 375 degrees.

LIGHT-AS-A-ZEPHYR YEAST ROLLS

1 package yeast
2 tablespoons warm water
¾ cup milk, scalded
¼ cup sugar

½ teaspoon salt
¼ cup butter, melted
2 eggs
2½ cups flour

Dissolve yeast in warm water. When milk has cooled to lukewarm, add sugar, salt, butter, eggs, and milk. Stir in flour all at once. Cover and refrigerate several hours or overnight. Remove from refrigerator two hours before time to bake. Roll out on floured surface to ½ inch thickness. Form into desired shape. Let rise two hours. Bake at 350 degrees until brown.

BUTTERMILK EGG BREAD

1 2/3 cups waterground
   cornmeal
1½ teaspoons salt
1 teaspoon soda

1½ teaspoons baking powder
2 beaten eggs
1 cup buttermilk
4 tablespoons butter

Sift dry ingredients together in large bowl. Beat eggs, add to buttermilk, and beat again. Pour into dry mixture and stir well. Melt butter in heavy skillet. Pour 2 tablespoons of the melted butter into batter and pour batter into skillet (the two tablespoons of butter remaining should be hot—as should skillet). Bake at 425 degrees until brown.

EGG BREAD

1 tablespoon shortening	1 cup flour
2 tablespoons sugar	2 tablespoons baking powder
2 beaten eggs	1 teaspoon salt
1 cup cornmeal	1 cup milk

Cream shortening and sugar and add beaten eggs. Stir in dry ingredients which have been sifted together. Add milk and stir again. Bake in greased iron skillet at 425 degrees until brown.

LADIES' LUNCHEON BANANA NUT BREAD

½ cup butter or margarine	2 eggs
1 cup sugar	2 cups flour
3 ripe bananas	Pinch salt
1 teaspoon soda	¾ cup chopped pecans
4 tablespoons buttermilk	

Cream butter and sugar well. Add bananas (they must be quite ripe) and mix well. Dissolve soda in buttermilk and add with eggs, flour, and salt. Mix well. Fold in pecans. Bake in one large or two small greased and floured loaf pans at 350 degrees for about 55 minutes. Cool before slicing. Serve with a fruit salad at a ladies' luncheon. If any bread is left, toast it with cheese for a breakfast treat.

APRICOT BREAD

1 cup dried apricots
¼ cup butter or margarine
1 cup sugar
1 egg
2 cups sifted flour

1¼ teaspoons baking powder
1 teaspoon soda
Pinch salt
1 cup orange juice
1 cup chopped pecans

Soak apricots in hot water at least 15 minutes, drain, and cut into small pieces. Cream butter and sugar and beat in egg. Sift dry ingredients together and fold in alternately with orange juice (may not need entire cup of juice). Fold in pecans and apricots. Bake in two small greased and floured loaf pans at 350 degrees about 50 minutes.

CREAM OF MUFFIN BREAD

½ cup shortening
¾ cup sugar
2 eggs
1 teaspoon salt

3 cups flour
3 teaspoons baking powder
1 cup milk

Cream shortening and sugar. Add eggs one at a time, beating well after each addition. Sift salt, flour, and baking powder together and add alternately with milk. If batter seems too stiff, add a bit more milk. Pour into greased baking pan and bake at 425 degrees. Cut in squares and serve hot with lots of butter, homemade preserves, and cold milk.

NUTTY BACON BREAD

8 to 10 strips bacon
1¼ cups flour
¾ cup cornmeal
3 teaspoons baking powder
½ teaspoon salt

1 cup milk
1 egg
¼ cup bacon drippings
½ cup chopped salted peanuts

Fry bacon crisp, drain well, cool, and crumble. Sift flour, meal, baking powder, and salt into large bowl. Mix together milk, egg, and bacon drippings, and add to dry ingredients. Mix only enough to moisten. Spread batter in greased 9-inch square pan. Sprinkle nuts and bacon over the top. Bake at 450 degrees for about 15 to 18 minutes. Serve hot. Mighty good with fresh vegetables or with a big green salad.

PINE HARBOR FIG BREAD

1 cup dried figs, cut up	1 teaspoon baking powder
2 tablespoons butter	½ teaspoon soda
1 cup honey	¾ cup milk
1 beaten egg	¼ cup buttermilk
2½ cups flour	1 cup chopped pecans
½ teaspoon salt	

Use figs that are soft. If they are hard, steam them to restore softness. Cream butter and honey until fluffy. Beat in egg. Sift dry ingredients together and add alternately with milk and buttermilk. Fold in figs and pecans. Spoon into greased and floured loaf pan and bake at 325 degrees for an hour and a quarter or until done.

GRANNY WHITE'S BROWN BREAD

½ cup molasses	2 teaspoons soda
1 beaten egg	1½ teaspoons salt
2 cups whole wheat flour	1/3 cup sugar
1 cup plain flour	2 cups buttermilk

Add molasses to beaten egg and mix well. Stir in whole wheat flour. Sift other flour, soda, salt, and sugar together and add alternately with buttermilk. Bake in greased and floured loaf pan at 375 degrees for about 45 minutes or until done.

GEORGIA PEANUT BREAD

3 cups flour
3 teaspoons baking powder
½ teaspoon soda
Big pinch salt
1 egg

¾ cup orange juice
¼ cup oil
1 1/3 cups orange marmalade
2 cups raw peanuts,
 shelled and husked

Sift flour, baking powder, soda, and salt together. Beat egg slightly and mix with orange juice and oil. Add to flour mixture. Stir to make smooth batter. Fold in marmalade and peanuts. Pour into greased and floured 9x5x3-inch loaf pan and bake at 350 degrees for an hour. Batter can also be divided and baked in two smaller pans, if desired. Baking time for the two loaves will not be quite so long as for the one big loaf.

SHORTENING BREAD

1 pound butter
1 cup light brown sugar

4 cups sifted flour

Have butter at room temperature so that flour and sugar can be mixed into it—hands are helpful! Place on floured surface and, using hands again, pat out until about half an inch thick. Cut into desired shapes and bake on cookie sheet at 325 degrees for 20 to 25 minutes. This bread would not have attained fame had it not been for the song ("Mammy's little baby loves short'nin', short'nin', Mammy's little baby loves short'nin' bread") written about it.

LOWNDES COUNTY MOLASSES BREAD

¼ cup sugar
½ cup molasses
¼ cup shortening, melted
1 egg, beaten until fluffy
2½ cups flour

1 teaspoon soda
2 teaspoons baking powder
½ cup buttermilk—maybe
 a little more

Add sugar, molasses, and shortening to beaten egg. Sift flour, soda, and baking powder together and add to egg mixture alternately with buttermilk. Bake in greased loaf pan at 350 degrees for about an hour.

TEATIME ORANGE BREAD

1 large orange
Boiling water
Chopped dates
½ cup sugar
2 tablespoons melted butter
1 teaspoon vanilla

1 slightly beaten egg
2 cups flour
1 teaspoon soda
1 teaspoon baking powder
Pinch salt
2/3 cup chopped pecans

Squeeze the juice from the orange into a measuring cup, and add enough boiling water to make one cup. Put the orange rind through the food chopper, and add enough raisins or chopped dates (perhaps a mixture of both) to make one cup. Put the watered juice and the fruit into a bowl. Add the sugar, melted butter, vanilla, and egg. Sift dry ingredients together. Sift again. Now add dry ingredients to liquids. Beat to blend well. Fold in nuts. Bake in greased and floured loaf pan at 350 degrees for an hour.

FAVORITE EGG BREAD

2 cups cornmeal
2 teaspoons salt
1 teaspoon soda

2 eggs
2 cups buttermilk or clabber
½ cup shortening

Sift meal, salt, and soda together in bowl. Beat eggs and add to dry mixture together with buttermilk. Beat well. Heat shortening in heavy skillet, and when it gets real hot, pour it on the batter and beat a little more. Then pour batter into hot skillet and bake in oven at 425 degrees until golden brown.

HERMITAGE SPOON BREAD

1 cup cornmeal
3 cups milk
3 tablespoons melted butter

1 teaspoon salt
1 teaspoon baking powder
3 well-beaten eggs

Put meal and milk in top of double boiler and cook over boiling water until it reaches the consistency of mush, about half an hour. Stir in butter, salt, and baking powder. Remove from heat. When it has cooled a bit, pour mixture slowly into beaten eggs and mix. Then pour whole thing into buttered casserole and bake at 375 degrees about 30 minutes or until top is brown. Serve immediately

HIGH COMPANY SPOON BREAD

2½ cups milk
½ cup cornmeal
2/3 teaspoon salt
2 teaspoons sugar
1 tablespoon melted butter

1 cup grated cheese
3 eggs, separated
½ teaspoon (generous)
 baking powder

Put milk in top of double boiler and heat. Stir in cornmeal and cook, stirring nearly all the time, until thick. Add salt, sugar, butter, and cheese. Turn off heat and stir until cheese melts. Remove from over boiling water. Beat egg yolks and stir in. When mush mixture cools somewhat, beat egg whites stiff, and fold in mixture with baking powder. Bake in buttered large casserole dish at 375 degrees for 40 or 45 minutes. Have diners assembled at table with silver poised when this is taken from oven.

HOE CAKE (MODERNIZED)

1 cup cornmeal
¾ teaspoon salt

Boiling water

To be made properly, of course, the blade of a well-used hoe and an open fire are needed. So is coarse, waterground cornmeal. Lacking these props, today's cook makes hoe cake by mixing the meal and salt in a shallow pan and putting it in the oven for a few minutes to make the meal crisp and bring out its flavor. Then put it in a bowl and moisten with enough boiling water so that it sticks together enough to be handled. Let stand about 45 minutes. Then shape by spoonfuls into flat cakes and fry on hot, greased skillet until brown.

CUSTARD-LIKE CORNBREAD

2 tablespoons butter
¾ cup cornmeal
¼ cup flour
1¼ teaspoons baking powder
¾ teaspoon salt
1½ cups plus 2 tablespoons milk
1 well-beaten egg

Melt butter in eight-inch square pan in 400 degree oven. Sift dry ingredients together and stir in the egg and one cup plus the two tablespoons of milk. Pour mixture into hot pan (do not let butter scorch, however!). Gently pour remaining ½ cup milk over batter in pan. Do not stir. Bake about 30 minutes. There will be a pan of soft, custardy bread begging to be eaten hot.

BUTTERMILK CORNBREAD, MOUNTAIN STYLE

4 tablespoons bacon grease
1 cup buttermilk
1 beaten egg
1 cup waterground cornmeal
1 teaspoon salt
½ teaspoon soda
2 teaspoons baking powder

Put bacon grease in heavy iron skillet, eight or ten inch size, and put it in 425 degree oven to heat. Mix buttermilk and egg together and sift in dry ingredients. Pour about half of hot grease from skillet into mixture. Stir. Then pour mixture into skillet and bake until lightly brown.

COUNTRY CRACKLING BREAD

1 cup cracklings
1½ cups cornmeal
4 tablespoons flour
1 teaspoon salt

1 teaspoon soda
1 beaten egg
1½ cups thick buttermilk
1 tablespoon melted bacon fat

Cracklings are not easy to come by these days. Those sold in stores are often so hard and dry they break teeth out even after they are soaked in hot water. However, satisfactory substitutes for the genuine cracklings can be made by trimming the fat off a ham or a pork roast, cutting it into small pieces, and browning it in a heavy skillet. Crisp bacon may also be substituted, but it is not quite the same as using cracklings.

Anyhow, the method is to sift the dry ingredients together and then stir in the cracklings. Beat the egg in the buttermilk and add. Have melted fat in hot skillet and pour in batter. Bake at 450 degrees until light brown.

CRACKLING PONES

Use basic crackling bread recipe (Country Crackling Bread) but use only enough buttermilk to make a stiff batter. Shape into small pones, place on a greased baking sheet, and bake at 375 degrees until brown.

LORENZO DOW JOURNEY (JOHNNY) CAKE

1¼ cups cornmeal
¾ cup flour
2/3 teaspoon salt
¾ teaspoon soda

2 cups buttermilk
2 eggs
2 tablespoons molasses

Sift first three ingredients into bowl. Stir soda into buttermilk until it foams and fizzes. Add to meal-flour mixture. Dump in eggs and molasses and stir well. Pour into well-greased skillet and bake at 400 degrees for about 20 minutes. This cake, bread really, travels well and was often baked to take on a journey. Hence its name.

SOUTHERN CORN STICKS

1 cup cornmeal
2 teaspoons baking powder
½ teaspoon soda
¾ teaspoon salt

1 cup buttermilk
1 unbeaten egg
3 tablespoons bacon drippings or
  melted butter

Grease iron corn stick pans well and put in 450 degree oven to heat. Sift dry ingredients into bowl and stir in buttermilk, egg, and drippings or melted butter. Spoon batter into hot corn stick pan and bake until brown, about 20 minutes.

PLANTATION CORNBREAD

1¾ cups cornmeal
½ cup flour
1 teaspoon salt
2½ teaspoons baking powder

1½ cups milk
2 beaten eggs
5 tablespoons shortening
  or bacon grease

Sift dry ingredients together. Combine milk and beaten eggs and stir into cornmeal mixture. Do not beat. Meantime, melt shortening or bacon grease in heavy skillet (this can be done on top of stove) and pour two or three tablespoons of the melted fat into the batter, stirring it in. Pour mixture into very hot skillet (the remaining grease should cover bottom) and bake at 425 degrees until golden brown.

For a real treat, butter slices while hot and eat at once, with or without accompaniment.

HOT WATER CORNBREAD

2 cups cornmeal   1 teaspoon salt
3 cups boiling water   1 tablespoon butter

Scald meal with boiling water. Such instructions seldom appear in modern recipes, but it is not a difficult procedure: just have the meal ready in an ample bowl, and pour the boiling water over it, stirring quickly. After the meal is scalded, add the salt and butter. The mixture will be stiff. Spread mixture in a well-greased, heavy, ten-inch pan. Bake about half an hour at 300 degrees. Then run it under the broiler to brown. Use waterground meal if available: this old style meal gives the bread a nutty flavor — and it needs it!

CRISPY CORN ROUNDS

1 cup cornmeal   ½ teaspoon salt
1 tablespoon fat, melted   1 cup boiling water

Mix all ingredients and shape into balls. A heaping teaspoon of the mixture is about right for each ball. Put the balls on a well-greased baking sheet, placing them about three inches apart. Then wet your fingers (not dripping) and pat each of the balls into thin rounds. Bake at 400 degrees about ten minutes. The thinner the patties, the crispier they'll be.

HUSH PUPPIES

1 cup cornmeal   ½ teaspoon salt
4 tablespoons flour   1 egg
1 teaspoon baking powder   1 cup thick buttermilk
¼ teaspoon soda   1 medium onion, chopped fine

There are almost as many ways to make hush puppies as there are fishermen who provide the fish which traditionally accompany this

Southern bread. This recipe is pretty basic. Sift the dry ingredients together. Beat the egg in the buttermilk and add. Stir in chopped onion. Drop by teaspoonfuls (do not drop in big chunks) into very hot, deep fat, preferably fat in which fish has been fried. Turn when brown. Drain on paper and eat as soon as they are cool enough to handle.

CORNMEAL BATTERCAKES

1 cup cornmeal
½ teaspoon soda
½ teaspoon salt

1 beaten egg
1¼ cups buttermilk

Sift meal with soda and salt. Mix egg and buttermilk together well. Stir into dry ingredients. Drop by spoonfuls onto hot, greased skillet. When cakes are brown on the bottom, turn them deftly so that the other side may brown. Serve immediately with plenty of butter and country syrup.

CORN DODGERS

1 cup cornmeal
   (waterground variety preferred)
½ cup sifted flour

1 teaspoon salt
1½ teaspoons bacon drippings
1 cup scalded milk

Combine cornmeal, flour, and salt. Add bacon drippings and milk and mix well. Drop by spoonfuls into hot shortening and fry until golden brown.

SLAP JACKS

1 cup boiling water
1 cup yellow cornmeal

Pinch salt
1 beaten egg

Pour boiling water over sifted meal and salt. Stir in egg. Drop by spoonfuls into deep, hot fat. When brown, lift out and drain. Serve with thick cane syrup.

BATTERCAKES

2 eggs
1 cup buttermilk
¼ cup cornmeal
¾ cup flour
½ teaspoon salt

1 teaspoon baking powder
1 tablespoon sugar
½ teaspoon soda mixed in
1 tablespoon hot water

Beat eggs in milk and add meal. Leave it alone a few minutes. Add other ingredients, mixing well but not beating. Drop by spoonfuls on hot, greased griddle. Serve with plenty of butter and country syrup.

HOT CAKES FOR A COLD MORNING

1 cup milk
2 tablespoons melted
  shortening
1 beaten egg

1½ cups flour
3 teaspoons baking powder
¼ teaspoon salt
1 tablespoon sugar

Combine milk and shortening with beaten egg. Then add dry ingredients, sifted together, and beat until smooth. Pour by spoonfuls onto hot, lightly greased griddle and have hungry folks ready to eat. Plenty of butter and cane syrup are fine with these hot cakes.

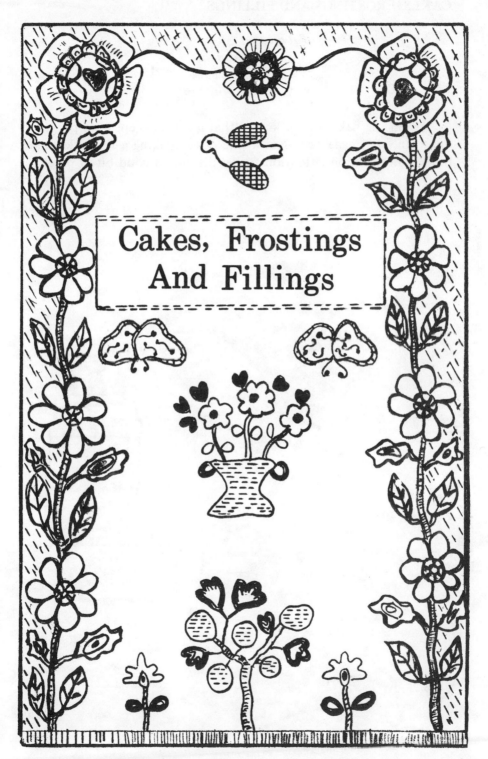

Cakes, Frostings
And Fillings

CAKES, FROSTINGS AND FILLINGS

Pat-a-cake, pat-a-cake,
Baker's man.
Bake me a cake
As fast as you can.

Even the baker's man knows that a cake, except for a packaged mix, can't be made fast. Not a fine cake. Making a fine cake takes time, concentration, attention to details, and a good bit of practice.

It also—or used to—requires cooperation from other members of the family. Generations of children grew up being admonished if they ventured into the kitchen during cake-making time, "Don't slam the door! And walk softly. Tiptoe. Don't shake the floor—the cake will fall!" Even the youngest child understood from the tone of voice that having the cake fall would be a disaster of the direst kind.

All across the South, cakes were revered as the sublime example of the baker's art. The most sought-after blue ribbon at the county fair was the one given for the best cake, and few compliments could surpass the accolade, "She's the best cake-maker in town."

Cakes are a customary accompaniment to any major Southern gathering: birthday parties, family reunions, weddings, church suppers, bridge luncheons, even funerals. Those cakes range from unadorned pound cake (still the queen of cakes to many Southern tastes) to elaborately decorated creations embellished with garlands of sugar rosebuds and leaves, dainty icing latticework, and entwined initials.

Those very fancy cakes were generally prepared only for weddings, although occasionally a special birthday or anniversary would merit such a masterpiece. Nearly every town had its wedding-cake specialist, an artist whose canvas was a perfect white cake and whose medium was boiled icing squeezed from a funnel of heavy white paper. In our town, Miss Bettie was that artist.

Young brides-to-be, even before their engagements were publicly announced, would hurry to Miss Bettie to ask her to make their wedding cakes. Somehow a wedding without one of Miss Bettie's cakes wouldn't seem proper: it would almost be like living in sin.

Miss Bettie never expected payment for making the cakes (she would have been offended by the offer of money), though the request for a cake was generally accompanied by the promise that "Mama said she'll send you plenty of fresh eggs and butter." Miss Bettie's cakes required lots of both.

Most memorable cakes do.

TRADITIONAL SOUTHERN CHOCOLATE CAKE

1 6-ounce package semi-sweet
   chocolate pieces
½ cup butter
4 well-beaten egg yolks
2/3 cup sugar, halved
1 cup sifted cake flour

1½ teaspoons baking powder
½ teaspoon soda
Pinch salt
½ cup milk
1 teaspoon vanilla
2 egg whites, beaten stiff

Put chocolate and butter in top of double boiler and melt over hot water. Put beaten egg yolks in large bowl (they can be beaten in this bowl—saves dish washing), add 1/3 cup sugar and beat until very thick. Sift dry ingredients together and add alternately with milk, beating until smooth. Stir in chocolate mixture and vanilla. Gently beat remaining 1/3 cup of sugar into stiff egg whites. Fold into batter. Carefully pour batter into two 8-inch layer pans which have been lined with paper. Bake at 350 degrees about half an hour. Cool. Cover with chocolate frosting or with a standard white icing.

DEVIL'S FOOD CAKE

5 tablespoons cocoa
1 egg yolk
1½ cups milk
½ cup butter, softened
2 cups sugar
2 eggs

2 cups sifted flour
2 teaspoons baking powder
¼ teaspoon soda
¼ teaspoon salt
1 teaspoon vanilla

Put cocoa, egg yolk, and one cup of milk in saucepan. Cook over medium heat, stirring constantly, until smooth and thick. Cream butter and sugar, add the two whole eggs and beat until fluffy. Blend in thickened cocoa mixture. Sift dry ingredients together and add alternately with remaining ½ cup of milk, beating smooth after each addition. Stir in vanilla. Pour into two 9-inch cake pans (bottoms lined with paper) and bake at 350 degrees about 25 minutes.

HONEY CHOCOLATE CAKE

¼ cup butter, softened
¾ cup sugar
½ teaspoon vanilla
2 eggs, separated
4 squares unsweetened
   chocolate, melted
2/3 cup honey

2 cups sifted cake flour
1 teaspoon baking powder
½ teaspoon soda
¼ teaspoon salt, heaping
½ cup buttermilk
½ cup milk, scalded

Cream butter with ½ cup sugar (save other ¼ cup sugar for later use). Add vanilla and mix well. Beat in egg yolks and melted chocolate. Blend in honey, adding gradually. Sift flour, baking powder, soda, and salt together and add alternately with buttermilk. Beat until smooth. Beat egg whites until stiff (not dry) and gradually add ¼ cup sugar (that's the sugar saved earlier—remember?), beating until glossy and very stiff. Fold into batter. Stir in scalded milk. Bake in two 9-inch layer pans which have been lined with paper (bottoms only) at 350 degrees for about half an hour.

DELICATE CHOCOLATE CHIFFON CAKE

1¾ cups sifted cake flour
¾ teaspoon soda
½ teaspoon salt
1½ cups sugar
1/3 cup salad oil

1 cup buttermilk
2 eggs, separated
2 squares unsweetened
   chocolate, melted

Sift flour, soda, salt, and one cup of sugar (that's not all the sugar called for!) together. Add oil and ½ cup buttermilk. Beat one minute. Add remaining buttermilk, egg yolks, and melted chocolate. Beat another full minute. Beat egg whites (two) until stiff and add remaining sugar (½ cup), beating until stiff. Fold into batter. Bake in two 8-inch layer pans (line bottoms with paper) at 350 degrees for half an hour.

BROWN VELVET CAKE

2 eggs
1¼ cups sugar
1½ cups sifted cake flour
1¼ teaspoons soda
¾ teaspoon salt

½ cup cocoa
2/3 cup salad oil
1 cup buttermilk
1¼ teaspoons vanilla

Beat eggs until thick and very yellow. Gradually beat in sugar. In separate bowl, sift dry ingredients and add oil, buttermilk, and vanilla. Beat until smooth. Fold gently but thoroughly into egg mixture. Bake in two 9-inch cake pans (bottoms lined with paper) at 350 degrees for 35 or 40 minutes.

$100 (BEFORE INFLATION) CHOCOLATE CAKE

½ cup butter or margarine
2 cups sugar
4 squares unsweetened
   chocolate, melted
2 eggs, separated

2½ cups sifted flour
2 teaspoons baking powder
1½ cups milk
½ teaspoon vanilla

Cream butter and sugar. Stir in melted chocolate and add beaten egg yolks. Sift flour and baking powder together and add alternately with milk. Fold in egg whites which have been beaten stiff and gently add vanilla. Bake in two oiled and floured layer pans at 350 degrees for 30 to 40 minutes. When cool, fill and frost with chocolate icing.

RED VELVET CAKE

1 cup shortening
1½ cups sugar
1 bottle red food coloring
   (1 ounce)
1¼ teaspoons vanilla
2 eggs

2 cups flour
1½ tablespoons cocoa
½ teaspoon salt
1 teaspoon vinegar
1 teaspoon soda
1 cup buttermilk

Beat shortening and sugar together until light and fluffy. Add food coloring, vanilla, and eggs and beat well. Sift flour, cocoa, and salt together more than once. Put vinegar and soda in buttermilk. Add flour and milk to creamed mixture a little at a time. Mix well. Pour batter into two greased and floured 9-inch cake pans and bake at 350 degrees for 30 or 35 minutes—watch carefully during final phase of baking. Cool and ice with a coconut icing.

FAMILY REUNION CARAMEL CAKE

½ cup butter
2 cups light brown sugar,
  packed
4 eggs, separated
1½ cups cake flour

1½ teaspoons baking powder
½ teaspoon salt
1/3 cup milk
1½ teaspoons vanilla
2/3 cup chopped nuts
  (optional)

Cream butter and sugar well. Add egg yolks singly, beating after each addition. Sift flour, baking powder, and salt together twice and add alternately with milk. Stir in vanilla and nuts, provided, of course, nuts are used. Now beat egg whites until stiff and fold into batter. Do this folding gently. Bake in two greased cake pans at 350 degrees for about 20 or 25 minutes. Remove from pans and cool on cake racks. Ice with:

Nutty Caramel Frosting

2 cups light brown sugar
1 cup half and half
3 tablespoons butter

1 teaspoon vanilla
1/3 cup chopped pecans

Mix sugar with half and half (or light cream) and cook over medium heat, stirring constantly until sugar dissolves. Then let mixture boil without stirring until it reaches the soft ball stage. Remove from heat. Stir butter in and then let cool. When cool, add vanilla and beat, beat, beat until icing gets thick and rich looking. Stir in nuts. Spread between layers and on top of cake. If too stiff, add a smidgen of cream to thin. Top may be decorated with pecan halves for added eye and taste appeal.

"HIGH COMPANY" LEMON CAKE

1/3 cup butter
2/3 cup shortening
2 cups sugar
3½ cups sifted cake flour

3 teaspoons baking powder
1 cup milk
6 egg whites
1 teaspoon vanilla

Cream butter, shortening, and sugar thoroughly. Sift dry ingredients together and fold in alternately with milk. Beat egg whites until stiff and fold in with vanilla. Avoid overbeating. Bake in three layer pans at 375 degrees for about 25 or 30 minutes. Let cakes cool while you make this filling:

Lemon Jelly Filling

1 cup sugar
3 tablespoons cornstarch
½ cup hot water

2 lemons (juice and
  grated rind)
6 egg yolks
2/3 stick butter

Combine sugar, cornstarch, hot water, and lemon rind and juice in top of double boiler over hot water. Beat egg yolks until fluffy and add gradually to mixture in boiler. Add butter. Cook over simmering, not boiling, water, stirring constantly, until thick enough to hold shape in spoon. Remove from heat and cool. Spread on layers of cake.

ORANGE BUTTER CAKE

½ cup butter
¾ cup sugar
1 whole egg
½ teaspoon vanilla
1½ teaspoons grated orange
  rind
1½ cups sifted cake flour

1½ teaspoons baking powder
Pinch salt
2 tablespoons orange juice
1/3 cup milk
Confectioners' sugar
Sweetened fresh fruit
  (peaches, orange sections,
  berries, etc.)

Cream butter and sugar in the usual thorough way. Add egg, vanilla, and grated orange rind, beating well. Sift flour with baking powder and salt. Stir orange juice into milk and add this to first mixture alternately with flour. Pour into tube pan which has been greased and floured. Bake at 350 degrees for 35 to 40 minutes. Remove from pan and cool. Dust with confectioners' sugar and fill center with fresh fruit at serving time.

SILVER SHEEN CAKE

2/3 cup butter, softened
1½ cups sugar
1½ teaspoons vanilla
2½ cups sifted cake flour
2½ teaspoons baking powder

2/3 cup milk
¼ teaspoon salt (heaping)
½ teaspoon cream of tartar
4 egg whites

Beat butter and sugar together until creamy. Beat in vanilla. Sift flour with baking powder and add to mixture alternately with milk. Beat until smooth. Add salt and cream of tartar to egg whites and beat until stiff (not dry). Fold into batter. Bake in two 9-inch layer pans lined with paper at 350 degrees for 25 to 30 minutes.

AFTERNOON TEA LAYER CAKE

½ cup butter or margarine
1 cup sugar
2 eggs
½ teaspoon grated orange
  rind
1 tablespoon orange juice

1½ cups sifted cake flour
1½ teaspoons baking powder
¼ teaspoon salt
½ cup water
Preserves
Confectioners' sugar

Cream butter and sugar until light. Add eggs, one at a time, and beat well after each addition. Stir in orange rind and juice. Sift flour, baking powder, and salt together and add alternately with water. Beat until smooth. Have two 9-inch cake pans lined with paper and ready. Divide the batter into the two pans. Bake at 350 degrees about 25 minutes. Remove from pans and cool. When cool, spread preserves (apricot preserves or orange marmalade is temptingly tangy) on one layer. Top with second layer. Sprinkle top layer with sifted confectioners' sugar.

APPALACHIAN STACK CAKE

Pioneer neighbors used to bake a layer for a stack cake to take to a wedding. The assembled layers became the bride's cake, and her popularity was judged by its height. The cake was cut and served at the newlyweds' wedding party or "infare," and in some parts of the South these stack cakes are called infare cakes.

½ cup butter (soft)
1½ cups sugar
2 slightly beaten eggs
4 cups flour
4 teaspoons baking powder

½ teaspoon soda
2/3 teaspoon salt
1 cup buttermilk
2 teaspoons vanilla

Cream butter and sugar. Add eggs and beat together well. Sift together 3¾ cups flour (save remaining ¼ cup), baking powder, soda, and salt. Add to creamed mixture alternately with buttermilk. Add vanilla. Mix all quickly to form soft dough (not batter). Divide into six parts. Use remaining flour to roll out each of the six parts so that it will fit into round, greased and floured pan. There will be six pans of cake to bake at 450 degrees. Remove from oven when lightly browned and spread layers with this apple filling:

1 pound dried tart apples
1 cup brown sugar
½ cup sugar

1½ teaspoons cinnamon
½ teaspoon allspice
½ teaspoon cloves

Cook apples until tender (cover with water and simmer). Drain and mash. Add sugar and spices and spread between layers of cake.

FRESH APPLE LAYER CAKE

1 cup shortening
2 cups sugar
3 eggs
2½ cups flour
1 teaspoon cinnamon
1 teaspoon soda

½ cup water
3 medium apples, peeled
  and cut up fine
1 cup chopped pecans
1 teaspoon vanilla

Cream shortening and sugar, beating well. Add eggs one at a time, beating after each one. Sift flour, cinnamon, and soda together and add alternately with water. Fold in chopped nuts and apples. Add vanilla. Pour into two greased and floured layer cake pans and bake at 350 degrees about 35 minutes or until cake begins to leave side of pans.

PURELY SOUTHERN COCONUT CAKE

1 cup shortening	3 teaspoons baking powder
2 cups sugar	½ teaspoon salt
4 eggs	1 cup milk
3 cups cake flour	1½ teaspoons vanilla

Cream shortening and sugar well. Add eggs, one at a time, beating between each addition. Sift flour, baking powder, and salt together and add alternately with milk which has vanilla stirred into it. Be sure last addition is of flour. Divide into three equal portions, put in three greased and floured pans, and bake at 375 degrees about half an hour. Cool for five minutes before removing from pan. While still in pan, pierce each layer in several places with the tines of a fork (two-tine kitchen fork is fine for this), and spoon a little coconut milk over each layer.

When cool, frost with this concoction:

1½ cups sugar	1 tablespoon white corn syrup
2 egg whites	3 drops vinegar
4 tablespoons water	1 teaspoon vanilla

Put everything except vanilla in top of double boiler. Use hand electric mixer or rotary beater to beat constantly for seven minutes while this mixture cooks over hot water. Beat until it forms peaks—this may take longer than seven minutes. Remove from heat and stir in vanilla. Frost cake and sprinkle generously with freshly grated coconut. Canned or frozen coconut may be used—but it will not be quite as good (also there will not be any coconut milk to moisten the layers of the cake)—and it will not be purely Southern.

49

EMMA'S OWN LANE CAKE

*The cake and filling are said to have been created by Mrs. Emma Rylander Lane, a resident of Barbour County, Alabama, in the late 1890s, but since her cookbook was published in Macon, Georgia, (*Some Good Things To Eat—1898*), Georgians lay claim to this fine cake recipe, too.*

1 cup butter
2 cups sugar
3½ cups sifted flour
2½ teaspoons baking powder
Pinch salt

1 cup milk
2 teaspoons vanilla
8 egg whites beaten stiff
   (not dry)

Cream butter and sugar until light and fluffy. Sift flour, baking powder, and salt together three times. Stir vanilla into milk. Add flour to creamed mixture alternately with milk, ending with flour. Fold in beaten egg whites. Bake in three greased and floured cake pans at 350 degrees for about 25 minutes. Some cooks prefer to bake this in four layers. When cool, the layers are put together with this filling:

Emma's Own Lane Cake Filling

8 egg yolks, beaten
1 cup sugar
½ cup butter

½ cup bourbon or brandy
   (wine will do)
1 teaspoon vanilla
1 cup chopped raisins

Put egg yolks, sugar, and butter in top of double boiler and cook over hot water, stirring nearly all the time, until thick. Remove from heat. Slowly add "spirits," blending well, and then add vanilla and raisins. Spread between layers of cake. Although the original recipe called only for raisins, later variations call for the addition of 1 cup grated coconut and 1 cup chopped pecans to the filling.

JAM CAKE

1 cup butter or margarine
2 cups sugar
4 eggs
1 teaspoon soda
1 cup buttermilk

4 cups flour
1 teaspoon allspice
1 cup jam (strawberry,
    raspberry, etc.)

Cream butter and sugar and beat well together. Add eggs and beat some more. Dissolve soda in buttermilk. Sift dry ingredients together and add alternately with foaming milk. Beat well. Stir in jam. Pour batter into three 9-inch layer cake pans, oiled and floured, and bake at 350 degrees about 45 minutes. When layers are cool, put them together with buttermilk filling or a fruit filling.

LADY BALTIMORE CAKE

Owen Wister may have been visiting in Georgia when he wrote in his novel Lady Baltimore, *"She brought me the cake, and I had my first felicitous meeting with Lady Baltimore. Oh, my goodness! Did you ever taste it? It's all soft, and it's in layers, and it has nuts—but I can't write any more about it; my mouth waters too much."*

½ cup butter
1 cup sugar
1¾ cups flour
2 teaspoons baking powder

Pinch salt
½ cup rich milk
1½ teaspoons vanilla
4 egg whites

Cream butter and sugar thoroughly. Sift flour, baking powder, and salt together several times and add alternately with milk. Stir in vanilla. Beat egg whites stiff and fold in. Bake in two greased and floured pans at 350 degrees for about 25 minutes. Cool. Put layers together with seven-minute icing to which chopped dried figs, chopped seedless raisins, and nuts (pecans, almonds, or walnuts) have been added.

SPICY MOLASSES CAKE

½ cup sugar
1 cup molasses
¾ cup shortening, melted
2 beaten eggs
2½ cups flour
1 teaspoon soda

1 teaspoon baking powder
1 teaspoon allspice
1 teaspoon cinnamon
1 teaspoon cloves
1 cup boiling water

Combine sugar, molasses, and shortening. Add eggs. Sift in dry ingredients and pour in boiling water. Mix well. Pour into two greased and floured cake pans and bake at 350 degrees about 35 minutes. Serve warm with whipped cream flavored with bourbon. Or eat it plain. Or cover squares with applesauce.

PRISSY'S PRUNE CAKE

½ cup shortening
1 cup sugar
2 eggs
1½ cups sifted flour
2/3 teaspoon baking powder
½ teaspoon soda

½ teaspoon salt
¼ teaspoon nutmeg
½ teaspoon allspice
½ teaspoon cinnamon
2/3 cup buttermilk
2/3 cup stewed prunes

Cream shortening and sugar until light. Add eggs, one at a time. Sift dry ingredients together twice and add alternately with buttermilk to creamed mixture. Beat after each addition. Fold in prunes (be sure no pits remain!). Bake in two greased and floured cake pans for about half an hour.

OLD STAND-BY WHITE LAYER CAKE

1 cup butter
2 cups sugar
3½ cups flour
3 teaspoons baking powder

Pinch salt
1 cup rich milk
1 teaspoon vanilla
6 egg whites, beaten stiff

Beat butter until fluffy and gradually add sugar, beating every minute. Sift dry ingredients together and add to butter mixture alternately with milk. Stir in flavoring (some cooks prefer almond or lemon extract instead of vanilla – use what you choose). Gently fold in beaten egg whites. Pour batter (spooning it is easier) into two greased and floured cake pans for thick layers or into three such pans for thinner layers. Bake at 350 degrees 25 to 30 minutes.

PECAN CAKE

1 cup shortening	1 teaspoon soda
2 cups sugar	1½ teaspoons cinnamon
4 beaten eggs	½ teaspoon ground cloves
3 cups sifted flour	1 cup buttermilk
1 teaspoon baking powder	2 cups chopped pecans

Cream together shortening and sugar. Stir in beaten eggs. Sift dry ingredients together and add alternately with milk. Beat. Fold in pecans. Bake in greased tube pan at 350 degrees for an hour. This cake needs no frosting.

PERSIMMON CAKE

Mighty few people will ever come by two cups of wild persimmon pulp, but for those who do (please be sure the persimmons are real, real ripe!), here is how to make a genuine persimmon cake:

2½ cups brown sugar	2 teaspoons allspice
2/3 cup shortening	2 teaspoons soda
3 whole eggs	2 cups persimmon pulp
2½ cups flour	2 cups raisins
2 teaspoons cinnamon	2 cups chopped pecans

Cream sugar and shortening, add eggs, and beat until fluffy. Sift dry ingredients together and add. Stir in persimmon pulp. Fold in raisins and pecans. Bake in oiled and floured tube pan at 250 degrees for about two hours. Probably longer.

ORANGE COCONUT LAYER CAKE

1 cup shortening
2 cups sugar
½ teaspoon vanilla
4 eggs

3 cups sifted cake flour
2½ teaspoons baking powder
¾ teaspoon salt
1 cup milk

Cream shortening and add sugar gradually, beating until light and fluffy. Add vanilla. Add eggs, one at a time, beating well after each addition. Sift flour, baking powder, and salt together and add alternately with milk. Mix until smooth. Pour batter into three cake pans which have been lined with paper and greased. Bake at 350 degrees about 25 minutes. Let stand in pans for five minutes after removing from oven, and then turn out on cake racks to cool. Spread Orange Filling between layers and Coconut Frosting on top.

Orange Filling

½ cup sifted cake flour
1 cup sugar
¼ teaspoon salt
¼ cup water
1¼ cups orange juice

¼ cup lemon juice
2 tablespoons grated
  orange rind
1 grated lemon rind
4 egg yolks

To make orange filling, mix flour, sugar, salt, and water in heavy saucepan and stir until smooth. Add the juices and the grated rinds and cook over low heat until mixture thickens and becomes almost transparent. Beat the egg yolks slightly and slowly pour the hot mixture over them, stirring constantly. Return to saucepan and cook, continuing to stir constantly, slowly for about five minutes or until mixture thickens again. Cool before spreading on cake.

Coconut Frosting

1½ cups sugar
½ teaspoon cream of tartar
Pinch salt
½ cup hot water

½ cup egg whites
¼ teaspoon vanilla
2 cups fresh grated coconut

54

The coconut frosting is made by combining sugar, cream of tartar, salt, and water in saucepan and cooking, without stirring, until a little dropped in cold water forms a soft ball (240 degrees on candy thermometer). Beat egg whites until stiff but not dry. Add hot syrup slowly to egg whites, beating rapidly with rotary beater or with electric mixer at high speed. Add flavoring. Spread frosting on top and sides of cake. Sprinkle generously with coconut.

APRICOT-PRUNE UPSIDE-DOWN CAKE

¼ cup butter
½ cup brown sugar
¾ teaspoon grated lemon
  rind
10 apricot halves (cooked)
10 prune halves (cooked)
1/3 cup shortening

2/3 cup sugar
1 beaten egg
1 cup milk
2 cups sifted cake flour
3 teaspoons baking powder
¼ teaspoon salt
½ teaspoon vanilla

Blend butter, sugar, and lemon rind and spread over bottom of greased 8-inch cake pan. Arrange apricot and prune halves (this is dried variety) atop mixture.

Cream shortening and sugar well. Add egg, beating until fluffy. Sift dry ingredients together and add alternately with milk. Stir in vanilla. Spoon over fruit in pan. Bake at 350 degrees for 40 minutes. Turn onto serving platter.

OLD-TIMEY POUND CAKE

1 pound butter
3½ cups sugar
4 cups sifted flour
1 teaspoon baking powder

Pinch salt
12 whole eggs
3 teaspoons vanilla

Cream butter and sugar until fluffy. Sift flour, baking powder, and salt together and add gradually to creamed mixture with an egg or two being added between each batch of dry ingredients. Beat well all the time. Stir in vanilla. Bake in two greased and floured tube pans for an hour at 350 degrees.

HERMIT CAKE

1 cup butter
1½ cups brown sugar
3 egg yolks
Juice ½ fresh lemon
1 pound chopped dates
½ pound chopped English
   walnuts

2 teaspoons vanilla
½ teaspoon nutmeg
½ teaspoon cinnamon
2½ cups flour
1½ teaspoons baking powder
3 egg whites, stiffly
   beaten

Cream butter and sugar and add egg yolks one at a time, stirring well after each addition. Squeeze lemon juice over chopped dates, add nuts, and combine well. Mix into creamed mixture and stir in vanilla. Sift nutmeg, cinnamon, flour, and baking powder together and add to creamed mixture alternately with stiffly beaten egg whites. Fold in gently but well. Bake in oiled and floured tube pan about two and one-half hours, maybe three, at 250 degrees. Put pan of water on bottom rack of oven (cake will be on second rack) for first two hours of baking.

TROPICAL CHIFFON CAKE

2¼ cups sifted cake flour
3 teaspoons baking powder
¾ teaspoon salt
1½ cups sugar
½ cup corn oil
6 large eggs, separated

2 large ripe bananas,
   sieved
1½ teaspoons grated orange
   rind
1/3 cup orange juice
½ teaspoon cream of tartar

Sift dry ingredients into mixing bowl. Make well in center of dry ingredients and fill this well with corn oil, egg yolks, banana, grated orange rind, and orange juice. Beat, using wooden spoon, until smooth.

Put egg whites in large bowl, add cream of tartar and beat until stiff peaks are formed. Fold into batter, mixing well. Pour into ungreased 10-inch tube pan and bake at 325 degrees about an hour and 10 or 15 minutes. Invert pan and cool completely. Remove from pan (leave bottom side up) and frost.

BROWN SUGAR NUT CAKE

1 cup butter, softened
½ cup margarine, softened
1 pound light brown sugar
1 cup sugar
3 cups flour

2 teaspoons baking powder
5 eggs
1 cup milk
1 teaspoon vanilla
1½ cups chopped pecans

Cream butter, margarine, and two sugars. Sift flour and baking powder together and add to creamed mixture alternately with eggs and milk. When well mixed, stir in vanilla and nuts. Bake in tube pan for an hour and a half at 325 degrees. This cake may be covered with a white icing if desired, but it really needs nothing extra done to it.

NUTTY APPLE CAKE

1¼ cups salad oil
2 cups sugar
3 eggs
2 teaspoons vanilla
3 cups flour

1 teaspoon soda
1 teaspoon salt
3 cups tart apples, diced
1 cup chopped pecans

Cream oil and sugar. Add eggs and vanilla, beating quite well. Sift flour with soda and salt. Add slowly. This mixing is more satisfactory if done with a sturdy spoon rather than with an electric mixer. Fold in diced apples and nuts. Bake in tube pan at 300 degrees for about an hour and a quarter or until done.

While still hot, glaze cake with one stick of butter, one cup of brown sugar, and 1/3 cup milk which have been boiled together for three or four minutes.

FIG PRESERVES CAKE

1 cup salad oil
2 cups sugar
3 eggs
2 cups flour
1 teaspoon soda
1 teaspoon allspice

1 teaspoon cinnamon
1 teaspoon nutmeg
2/3 cup buttermilk
1 cup fig preserves,
    undrained
1 cup chopped pecans

Cream oil and sugar. Add eggs one at a time, beating after each addition. Sift dry ingredients together and add alternately with buttermilk. Stir in fig preserves and nuts. Bake in tube pan at 350 degrees for about an hour or until done.

COFFEE CAKE

½ cup shortening
¾ cup sugar
1 teaspoon vanilla
3 eggs
2 cups sifted flour
1 teaspoon baking powder
2 teaspoons cinnamon

1 teaspoon soda
½ pint sour cream
6 tablespoons butter,
    softened
1 cup brown sugar,
    firmly packed
1 cup chopped pecans

Cream shortening and sugar until fluffy. Add vanilla. Add eggs one at a time, beating after each addition. Sift flour, baking powder, and soda together and add to creamed mixture alternately with sour cream. Blend well after each addition. Spread half of batter in tube pan that has been greased and floured and lined on bottom with waxed paper. Mix butter, brown sugar, and cinnamon together until smooth and add nuts. Put half of this mixture over batter in pan. Spoon on remaining batter and cover it with butter-sugar mixture that is left. Bake a little less than an hour at 350 degrees. Cool cake in pan ten minutes before removing and inviting folks to sample its goodness.

APRICOT COFFEE CAKE

½ cup butter, softened
1 cup sugar
1 egg
1 cup sour cream
1½ cups flour
1 teaspoon baking powder
1 teaspoon soda

¼ teaspoon salt
1 teaspoon vanilla
½ cup apricot preserves
1 tablespoon sugar
1 teaspoon cinnamon
1 tablespoon butter,
softened

Cream together butter and 1 cup sugar. Add egg and sour cream and blend well. Sift flour, salt, baking powder, and soda together and stir in. Add vanilla.

Spread apricot preserves in bottom of greased loaf pan. Spoon batter over preserves. Combine 1 tablespoon sugar, cinnamon, and butter, mixing well, and sprinkle over batter. Bake at 350 degrees about 35 minutes.

HONEY NUT CAKE

1 cup sugar
½ cup salad oil
4 eggs
Grated rind 1 lemon
2 cups honey

½ teaspoon soda
3¾ cups sifted flour
2 teaspoons baking powder
½ teaspoon salt
1 cup chopped pecans

Beat sugar, oil, eggs, and lemon rind together until creamy. Heat honey almost to boiling point (don't let it boil!), remove from heat, and beat in soda. Add hot honey to first ingredients. Sift dry ingredients together, add to first mixture, and beat until blended. Stir in nuts. Bake in 9x13x2-inch pan lined with waxed paper, in 350 degree oven about an hour. Turn out on wire rack, remove paper, and let stand until cool. Store in airtight container for several days before serving. May be served plain or with a lemon sauce.

CINNAMON FLUFF

½ cup margarine
2/3 cup sugar
2 eggs
1½ cups sifted flour
2 tablespoons cinnamon
1 teaspoon baking powder
1 teaspoon soda

½ teaspoon salt
1 cup sour milk
  (buttermilk)
½ cup sugar
1 tablespoon butter
1 tablespoon cinnamon

Mix margarine, sugar, and eggs thoroughly, creaming until fluffy. Sift next five dry ingredients together and add alternately with sour milk. Pour batter into greased and floured pan. Mix remaining sugar, butter, and cinnamon together and sprinkle over top of batter. Bake at 350 degrees about 40 minutes. Serve hot.

SAVANNAH BOURBON CAKE

¾ cup butter
2 cups sugar
6 whole eggs
½ cup molasses
4 cups flour
2 teaspoons baking powder
1½ teaspoons cinnamon
  (or nutmeg)

1 pound seedless raisins
1 cup candied pineapple,
  chopped
1 cup candied cherries,
  chopped
2½ cups chopped pecans
1 cup orange marmalade
1 spilling-over cup fine
  bourbon

Cream butter and sugar. Add eggs, beating well after each egg is added. Pour in molasses and mix. Sift flour, baking powder, and spice together. Put the fruits and nuts in a large bowl with the marmalade, and put in about a cup of the flour mixture to coat these ingredients well—it will take some stirring to do this. Add remaining three cups of flour to creamed mixture, making the additions alternately with the bourbon. Stir in the floured fruits and nuts.

Grease two large loaf pans and line them with heavy brown paper which has been greased and floured. Pour batter into the prepared pans, spooning it well into the corners, and cover each pan with greased brown paper, oily side down. Bake in slow 250 degree oven until straw inserted in center comes out clean, about 2½ to 3 hours. These cakes need to ripen, so wrap each one in a white cloth which has been well dampened with bourbon and put it in a metal container with a tight lid. Put an apple in each container before closing the lid. In about three weeks—a month, if impatience can be curbed—the cakes are ready for slicing and eating. These cakes will keep almost indefinitely.

FUDGY SPICE CUPCAKES

1/3 cup shortening	½ teaspoon soda
1 cup sugar	1 teaspoon baking powder
1 teaspoon vanilla	1¼ teaspoons cinnamon
2 eggs	¼ teaspoon salt
2 squares unsweetened	½ cup hot water
chocolate, melted and cooled	½ cup buttermilk
2 cups sifted cake flour	½ cup molasses

Cream shortening and sugar. Add vanilla and mix well. Add eggs, one at a time, beating vigorously after each addition. Blend in melted chocolate. Sift dry ingredients together and add alternately with liquids, beating smooth after each addition. Fill greased cupcake pans half full of batter and bake at 350 degrees about 25 minutes.

PO' MAN'S FRUITCAKE

1 small package mincemeat	1 tablespoon mixed spice
1 pound seedless raisins	(ground)
1 cup shortening	2 teaspoons soda
1½ cups sugar	4 cups flour
2½ cups boiling water	1 cup chopped nuts

Combine mincemeat, raisins, shortening, sugar, water, and spices in heavy saucepan and boil together for 15 minutes, stirring all the while to prevent burning or scorching. Remove from heat and cool. Add to cooled mixture the soda, flour, and nuts. Bake in greased and floured loaf pan at 350 degrees for two hours.

MERRY CHRISTMAS FRUITCAKE

1½ cups candied cherries
½ cup candied citron, diced
1¼ cups seedless raisins
1 1/3 cups dried figs,
    chopped
1½ cups chopped pecans
2 cups flour
1 cup butter
1 cup sugar

5 eggs
¼ cup dark molasses
¼ cup brandy—good and
    strong
1 teaspoon soda
¾ teaspoon ground
    cinnamon
¼ teaspoon ground cloves
¼ teaspoon ground nutmeg

Put fruits and nuts in mixing bowl, and sift over them 1 cup flour. Use fingers to separate pieces of fruit so that each one is covered with flour. Cream butter and sugar well, using another bowl, of course. Add eggs one at a time, beating after each addition. Stir in molasses and brandy. Add remaining flour which has been sifted with soda and spices. Stir to blend. Fold in floured fruit-nut mixture. Bake in 9-inch angel food cake pan which has been lined with oiled foil. Bake at 300 degrees for two and a quarter hours or until done. Cool on wire rack. When completely cold, sprinkle with about 1/3 cup brandy, maybe more. Wrap in plastic, then in foil, and let stand at room temperature overnight.

WHITE FRUITCAKE

1 cup homemade wine
¼ pound citron, chopped
¼ pound candied cherries,
    chopped
¼ pound candied pineapple,
    chopped
1 pound butter
2 cups sugar

16 egg whites, beaten stiff
4 cups sifted flour
2 teaspoons baking powder
1 grated coconut
½ pound English walnuts,
    chopped
1 pound blanched almonds,
    chopped

Pour wine over fruits in bowl and let stand to soak up flavor. Cream butter and sugar. Beat egg whites well and add to creamed mixture alternately with flour which has been sifted twice with baking powder—save about a cup of this flour to use in coating the fruits. Stir in coconut. Drain wine from fruits (save it) and put the fruits in a container with the flour saved earlier, mixing them around until well coated with flour. Stir them into the batter. If it is too stiff to handle well, add some of the wine. Fold in the nuts last. Bake in three or four, depending on size, loaf pans which have been well oiled and floured. A heavy brown paper, well oiled, in the bottom of the pans is safer. Bake at 275 degrees for two hours. Test then (insert straw) to see if cakes are done. If not, continue baking. After the cakes are taken from the oven and removed from pans, pour the remaining wine, if any remains, over them while they are hot. When cool, they may be wrapped in wine-dampened cloths and stored in air-tight containers to mellow or ripen if desired.

OLD-FASHIONED BOILED ICING

3 egg whites
Pinch salt
¾ cup sugar

3 tablespoons water
1/3 cup white corn syrup
1½ teaspoons vanilla

Let egg whites come to room temperature. Put them and salt into bowl and beat until soft peaks form. Mix sugar, water, and corn syrup in a saucepan and bring the mixture to a boil, stirring constantly. Then boil without stirring until the syrup is thick enough to spin a fairly long thread (242 degrees on a candy thermometer, a gadget unheard of by most cooks who used this recipe). Remove from heat. Beat the egg whites again to high peak stage and slowly, very slowly, pour the hot syrup into them. Add the vanilla. Beat until the icing holds stiff peaks.

CREAM CHEESE FROSTING

1 8-ounce package cream
  cheese, softened
¼ cup margarine
1 box confectioners' sugar,
  sifted

1 teaspoon vanilla
1 cup chopped pecans

Beat cream cheese and margarine together until smooth. Add confectioners' sugar and mix well. Beat in vanilla. Spread between layers and on sides and top of cake. Sprinkle with chopped pecans.

PERFECT CARAMEL FILLING

3 cups sugar
3 tablespoons butter
1 cup thick buttermilk

¼ teaspoon soda
½ teaspoon vanilla
Pinch salt

Combine 2½ cups sugar, soda, and buttermilk in large pan. Melt the remaining ½ cup sugar in heavy iron skillet, stirring constantly. Add melted sugar to first mixture and boil until it reaches the soft ball stage. Remove from heat. Add vanilla, salt, and butter, and beat until thick enough to spread over cake.

ORANGE BUTTER FROSTING

¼ cup butter
1 egg yolk
Pinch salt
2 teaspoons lemon juice
Grated rind 1 lemon

Grated rind 1 orange
1 box confectioners' sugar, sifted
¼ cup orange juice

Cream butter until light. Add egg yolk, salt, and lemon juice. Beat well. Add grated rinds of fruits. Beat in confectioners' sugar, adding alternately with juice of orange. When smooth, spread on cake.

ORANGE COCONUT FILLING

3½ tablespoons cornstarch
1 cup sugar
½ cup orange juice
1 tablespoon grated orange rind
1 slightly beaten egg

3 tablespoons lemon juice
2 tablespoons butter
2 tablespoons water
¾ cup grated coconut

Combine everything except the coconut in a heavy saucepan and cook on low heat, stirring, until clear and thick, about 10 minutes. Cool. Stir in coconut. Spread between layers or on top of cake.

CHOCOLATE ICING

2 cups sugar
1 cup rich milk
1 package semi-sweet chocolate
  chips

15 large marshmallows
¼ cup butter

Combine sugar and milk and cook until it reaches the medium hard ball stage. Remove from heat and add chocolate chips, marshmallows, and butter. Beat hard until icing is of consistency to spread.

WHIPPED CREAM CHOCOLATE FROSTING

1½ cups whipping cream
¼ cup sugar

2½ tablespoons cocoa
½ teaspoon vanilla

Combine all ingredients in a bowl. Do not whip, just stir them together. Chill in refrigerator at least 2 hours. When well chilled, beat until mixture is so thick it stands in peaks. Remember, however, that you can beat too long and have chocolate butter, so be careful and not overdo the beating. Use for frosting cake destined for prompt eating. And be sure cake is completely cold before frosting is put on.

FUDGE FROSTING

2 tablespoons butter
2 squares unsweetened chocolate
Pinch salt
1 beaten egg

1 teaspoon lemon juice
1½ cups confectioners' sugar
1 teaspoon vanilla
½ cup chopped pecans, if desired

Melt butter and chocolate in top of double boiler. Remove from heat. Add other ingredients, mixing well. Spread on cake. Double this recipe for spreading between layers and on top of cake, too.

MOCHA FROSTING

½ cup butter, softened
1 box confectioners' sugar,
  sifted
1/3 cup powdered instant
  coffee
1 slightly beaten egg

2 tablespoons milk
1 square unsweetened chocolate,
  melted
Pinch salt
½ teaspoon vanilla

Cream butter and 1 cup sugar together well. Add next 6 ingredients and beat until smooth and creamy. Blend in remaining sugar.

MARSHMALLOW COCONUT ICING

1 cup sugar
1/3 cup water
8 large marshmallows

2 stiffly beaten egg whites
1 cup grated coconut

Mix sugar and water and cook over medium heat until it spins a thread. Add marshmallows and stir to melt them well. Fold into beaten egg whites. Spread over cooled cake layers and sprinkle with grated coconut.

COCONUT FROSTING

2 egg whites
1 cup white corn syrup
Pinch salt

1 teaspoon vanilla
1½ cups grated coconut

Put egg whites, syrup, and salt in top of double boiler over rapidly boiling water. Beat with rotary beater until mixture forms peaks. Remove from heat. Add vanilla and fold in gently. Spread on cake when cold. Sprinkle with grated coconut.

LEMON CHEESE FILLING

1 cup sugar
2½ tablespoons flour
Grated rind 1 lemon

¼ cup lemon juice
1 beaten egg
1 tablespoon butter

Mix flour and sugar together in top of double boiler. Add lemon juice and beaten egg and combine well. Cook over hot water, stirring constantly, until thick. Remove from heat. Stir in butter and grated lemon rind. Cool before spreading on cake.

Candy

CANDY

On living room tables throughout the South not too many years ago, boxes of candy (often Whitman's Sampler) shared space with the poems of James Whitcomb Riley and the novels of Harold Bell Wright. The boxes held what was called "beau candy," brought to young ladies by their gentlemen callers, and a young lady's popularity was often judged by the number and size of the candy boxes on display (it was considered proper to display only full or partially filled boxes).

When there was a surfeit of beau candy, particularly around Christmas or Valentine's Day, there sometimes developed a practice of spit-backs, not as vulgar as the name implies, in which family members selected a piece of candy and broke it in two to see if it was the kind they wanted. If they did not like the chosen piece and if no one else present at the time wanted it, the candy was pressed back together and placed in a box reserved for such rejects—or spit-backs. A week or so after all the favorite pieces of candy had been eaten, the box with the spit-backs was brought out. By then it was welcome.

Beau candy was subject to another hazard, too. Brothers (and even fathers) were known to lift out the top layer of a box of candy, eat the entire second layer, and then carefully replace the top layer. Such gluttonous thefts were seldom discovered until after the culprit had long escaped.

But beau candy, tempting though it is, cannot compare with the goodness and the variety of homemade Southern confections.

Making candy in Southern kitchens has always been a festive event, whether it be old-fashioned molasses pull candy ("Catch it quick before it falls on the floor!") or marshmallow creme fudge fancied up with nuts and cherries. And no girls' spend-the-night-party (a much more apt name than slumber party) would be proper without a late-night invasion of the kitchen to whip up a batch of chocolate candy. Strange, isn't it, how a crowd of hungry boys so often just happened along just as the candy got done!

MARSHMALLOW FUDGE

4 cups sugar
1 large can evaporated milk
½ cup butter
1 pint marshmallow creme

3 packages chocolate chips
3 cups chopped pecans
1½ teaspoons vanilla

Combine sugar, milk, and butter in large, heavy pan and cook over medium heat, stirring every second. Let boil for seven minutes. Remove from heat and immediately pour over marshmallow creme and chocolate chips (have them waiting in big bowl). Fold together well to mix. Stir in nuts and vanilla. This is supposed to be dropped by spoonfuls onto waxed paper, but this gets tiresome. Just pour it into buttered pans. When cool, cut into squares.

BUTTERMILK FUDGE

2 cups sugar
1 cup buttermilk
½ teaspoon soda
2 tablespoons white corn syrup

1 teaspoon butter
1½ teaspoons vanilla
1 cup chopped pecans

Combine first four ingredients in heavy saucepan and cook on medium heat, stirring often, until mixture begins to thicken. Then it is stir, stir, stir to prevent scorching. Cook to soft ball stage. Remove from heat, add final three ingredients, and begin beating at that instant. As soon as mixture begins to cream and thicken, pour it immediately onto a buttered platter. Cut candy into squares before it cools, but do not remove it from platter until it is cold and firm.

CHOCOLATE PEANUT STACKS

1 tablespoon butter
2 tablespoons cream
1 egg yolk

2 squares chocolate, melted
2¼ cups confectioners' sugar
1½ cups small peanuts

Cream butter. Add cream, egg yolk, melted chocolate, and mix well. Stir in enough sugar (may take a bit more) to make a stiff texture. Add peanuts, stirring to distribute well. Drop by spoonfuls onto buttered dish.

SATURDAY FUDGE

2 squares unsweetened chocolate
½ cup rich milk
1/3 cup light corn syrup
1½ tablespoons butter
   or margarine

2 cups sugar
1 teaspoon vanilla
1 cup chopped pecans (optional)

Put everything except vanilla and pecans (if they are used—and surely they will be!) in saucepan and cook over medium heat, stirring virtuously, until mixture boils. Continue cooking, stirring less constantly, until soft ball stage is reached. Remove from stove and let cool a little while. Stir in vanilla. Beat until fudge gets thick and loses its gloss. Stir in pecans (still assuming they are being used) and speedily pour into buttered pan. Cut in squares when cool. If a more definite chocolate fudge is desired, use three squares of unsweetened chocolate instead of two.

QUICK PEANUT BUTTER FUDGE

1/3 cup margarine
½ cup light corn syrup
¾ cup peanut butter
½ teaspoon salt

1 teaspoon vanilla
4½ cups sifted confectioners'
   sugar
¾ cup chopped nuts

In large mixing bowl, combine margarine, syrup, peanut butter, and vanilla. Add salt. Gradually stir in confectioners' sugar. Knead until well blended and smooth. Add nuts gradually. Use rolling pin to roll out into square ½ inch thick. Cut into serving pieces.

HAYSTACKS (CHOCOLATE MARSHMALLOW KIND)

1 3-ounce package cream cheese, softened
2 tablespoons milk
2 cups confectioners' sugar, sifted

2 ounces unsweetened chocolate, melted
½ teaspoon vanilla
Pinch salt
3 cups miniature marshmallows
½ cup flaked coconut (about)

Blend cream cheese and milk. Gradually add sugar. Stir in chocolate, vanilla, and salt. Fold in marshmallows. Drop by teaspoonfuls into flaked coconut, rolling each spoonful about until well coated. Place on cookie sheet and chill until firm.

CHOCOLATE NUT DROPS

1 6-ounce package semi-sweet chocolate
2/3 cup sweetened condensed milk
1 cup quick-cooking oatmeal (raw)

Pinch salt
1 teaspoon vanilla
5 dozen pecan halves

Put chocolate in top of double boiler and melt over hot water. Do not stir. When chocolate has melted, add other ingredients except pecans (be certain you use condensed milk—not evaporated milk) and stir until thoroughly mixed. Turn off heat but leave mixture over hot water while dropping by teaspoonfuls onto buttered cookie sheet. Press a pecan half on top of each piece. Put in refrigerator until firm.

TRADITIONAL CARAMEL CANDY

3 cups sugar
1 cup real cream
¼ teaspoon soda

¼ cup butter
1 teaspoon vanilla
1½ cups chopped pecans

Put one cup of sugar in heavy iron skillet over low heat. Stir with wooden spoon (do this constantly) until sugar melts and is light brown in color. Pour this caramelized sugar into saucepan in which are mixed cream and remaining sugar. Cook to firm ball stage, stirring every whipstitch. Take off stove and quickly add soda. Stir hard. Add butter. Do not stir. Cool for ten minutes. Add vanilla and beat until candy is thick. Fold in nuts. Spread in buttered pan and cut into squares. This candy can also be dropped by spoonfuls onto waxed paper.

RING-A-LING-LINGS

1 6-ounce package semi-sweet
  chocolate
1 cup cornflakes

1 teaspoon vanilla
1 cup salted peanuts
½ cup flaked coconut

Melt chocolate pieces over hot water. Add other ingredients and drop by teaspoonfuls onto waxed paper. Chill until firm.

PULLED CANDY

Pulling candy used to provide entertainment at rural parties with couples working together on the project.

3 cups sugar
¼ cup vinegar

½ cup water
2 tablespoons butter

Combine all ingredients except butter in heavy pan and cook slowly (do not stir this, for a change!) until test drops are brittle when dropped into cold water. Remove from heat, add butter, and pour out on buttered platter or slab. When cool enough to handle, butter fingers and thumbs generously, take up a hunk of the candy, and pull it with long, even strokes until it becomes light colored. The procedure is to pull and fold back, pull and fold back, pull and fold back. Put pulled portions on buttered platters to cool. When cold, a whack of a knife will break candy into pieces.

DIVINITY

2 cups sugar
½ cup white corn syrup
½ cup water
Pinch salt

2 egg whites, beaten stiff
1 teaspoon vanilla
½ cup chopped pecans

Combine sugar, corn syrup, water, and salt in saucepan. Stir until sugar is dissolved as mixture heats. Then let cook without stirring to the hard ball stage (252 degrees). Take from heat and pour slowly over stiffly beaten egg whites, beating constantly. Continue to beat until mixture is no longer glossy. Quickly stir in vanilla and pecans, and just as quickly drop candy from tip of teaspoon onto buttered platter. Do not try to make divinity if it is thundering or if the weather is damp.

VANILLA CARAMELS WITH NUTS

2 cups sugar
1 cup light corn syrup
½ teaspoon salt
2 cups rich milk

1/3 cup butter or margarine
1 teaspoon vanilla
2/3 cup chopped pecans

Put sugar, syrup, and salt in large saucepan and add one cup of the rich milk. Mix well. Cook, stirring constantly, for about ten minutes. Slowly add the remaining cup of milk, adding so slowly that the boiling does not stop. Continue cooking and stirring for five more minutes. Add the butter, a little bit at a time, stirring and stirring. Continue to cook mixture over low heat (continue stirring, too) until a small amount forms a firm ball when dropped in cold water. That is 248 degrees on a candy thermometer, if one is handy. Remove from heat. Gently mix in vanilla and nuts. Pour into well-buttered 8-inch square pan to cool. When cool, turn out on board and cut into squares. Wrap each piece in waxed paper, twisting the ends, or in plastic wrap.

Chocolate caramels may be made by adding three (four if you are a real chocolate fiend) squares of melted, unsweetened chocolate to the beginning mixture.

CARAMEL CANDY

2 cups sugar
1 cup brown sugar
3 tablespoons white corn syrup
Pinch salt

1 cup milk
1 tablespoon butter
½ teaspoon vanilla
1 cup chopped pecans

Stir the sugars, syrup, and salt together in saucepan with milk and cook on medium heat, stirring to prevent sticking, until it reaches the soft ball stage. Cool. Add butter and vanilla and begin beating. As candy thickens, add nuts. Pour onto buttered surface to cool.

PEANUT BRITTLE

3 cups sugar
1 cup white corn syrup
½ cup water

3 cups raw peanuts (Spanish type)
2 teaspoons soda

Put sugar, syrup, and water in heavy saucepan and cook over medium heat, stirring constantly, until sugar melts. Then do not stir any more but add peanuts and continue cooking until it reaches the hard crack stage (300 degrees). Before this stage is reached, have buttered platter or slab ready as it will be needed in a hurry. When the hard crack stage is reached, remove from heat, add baking soda, and stir quickly. Pour out on waiting buttered surfaces, pouring it thin. Cool. Break into pieces.

SUGARED PECANS

2 cups sugar
2/3 cup water

Grated rind 1 orange
1 quart shelled pecans

Mix sugar and water and boil together until syrup spins a thread, then continue cooking slowly until mixture reaches soft ball stage. Remove from heat. Add grated orange rind and stir until foamy. Stir in shelled pecans, being sure candy coats each one. Pour onto lightly greased dish. Nuts may be separated with two forks while candy is still warm or you may let candy cool and harden and then break into pieces.

PINE MOUNTAIN PRALINES

1 pound light brown sugar
1 small can evaporated milk
2 tablespoons light corn syrup

¼ cup margarine
1 teaspoon vanilla
1½ cups pecans (halves or large
    pieces)

Place sugar, milk, and corn syrup in saucepan and cook over medium heat, stirring diligently, until it comes to a boil. Continue cooking, stirring every now and then, until it reaches soft ball stage. Remove from heat and put in margarine but do not stir. When candy is lukewarm, pour in the vanilla and beat until it gets creamy. Stir in pecans. Fast. Drop by spoonfuls onto waxed paper. Use spoon to shape into circles and to spread out pecans. Leave candy alone until pralines are cool, firm, and sugared. Wrap each one separately before storing.

CANDIED ORANGE PEEL

6 oranges with thick,
    flawless skins
Water
1 teaspoon salt

2 cups sugar
½ cup light corn syrup
Additional sugar

Wash oranges and dry them. Cut into quarters and remove peelings. Put peels into large saucepan, cover with water, add salt, and boil for 20 minutes. Peel should be tender then. Drain. Cut peel into thin (¼-inch wide) strips. Put into saucepan 2 cups sugar, corn syrup, and 1 cup water. Cook over moderate heat, stirring steadily, until sugar dissolves. Add orange strips. Bring to boil again. Reduce heat so that a gentle boil continues. Cook for about 45 minutes. Most of syrup should have been absorbed by then. Pour into colander to drain. Sprinkle sugar generously on waxed paper. Roll orange strips in sugar. Place on cookie sheets and put in 150 degree oven for an hour to dry. Remove from oven and place on wire racks for about three hours. Arrange in layers, with waxed paper between each layer, in tightly covered metal box.

This same method is used for making candied grapefruit peel.

APRICOT DREAMS

1 pound dried apricots
1 orange with thick skin
Juice 1 orange

Juice 1 lemon
2 cups sugar
Pecan halves

Grind apricots and whole orange together. Add orange juice, lemon juice, and sugar. Mix. Cook over low heat, stirring until juice has cooked out. Cool. Drop from teaspoon into a mound of sugar. Roll into ball and place on waxed paper. Top each ball with a pecan half and let dry.

DATE ROLL

3¼ cups sugar
½ cup butter
1 large can evaporated milk
1 heaping cup chopped dates

Pinch salt
1 teaspoon vanilla
2 cups chopped pecans

Put sugar, butter, and milk in heavy container (a deep, cast iron pot is ideal) and cook over medium low heat until butter melts and sugar dissolves. Stir constantly. When mixture comes to a rolling boil, add dates. Cook, stirring all the while, until a soft ball is formed when a little bit of the boiling mixture is dropped into a cup of cold water. Remove from stove and beat with renewed vigor. Beat until the candy begins to get thick and stiff. Quickly add salt, vanilla, and nuts. Stir. When cool enough to handle, shape into a roll and wrap in kitchen towel (cotton) which has been dipped in cold water and then wrung nearly dry. Allow to cool completely before slicing. Leave towel wrapped around roll and add a wrapping of aluminum foil to preserve freshness and to assist in ripening. This confection should not be refrigerated.

QUICK APRICOT NUT BALLS

1½ cups dried apricots, ground
1 2/3 cups shredded coconut
2/3 cup ground pecans

1 cup sweetened condensed milk
Confectioners' sugar

Mix apricots, coconut, and pecans with condensed milk. Shape into marble-sized balls (make the marbles rather large—taws, not peewees), roll in confectioners' sugar, and allow to dry on wire racks.

STUFFED PRUNES

1 cup coconut, flaked
1 cup pecans
¼ cup honey

2 teaspoons fresh lemon juice
3 dozen prunes, pitted,
cooked, and drained

Put coconut and pecans through food chopper. Mix well with honey and lemon juice. Stuff prune centers with mixture. May be rolled in confectioners' sugar, if desired.

OLD-FASHIONED POPCORN BALLS

1 cup light corn syrup
1 cup brown sugar,
firmly packed
¼ cup water

1 teaspoon vinegar
2 tablespoons margarine or
butter
2 quarts popped corn
(unsalted)

Mix syrup, sugar, water, and vinegar in saucepan and bring to boil over medium heat, stirring constantly. Cook, stirring frequently, until it reaches stage that a small sample dropped into cold water forms a ball hard enough to hold its shape (260 degrees on candy thermometer). Remove from heat and stir in butter. Slowly pour over popped corn in large bowl, stirring to mix well while pouring. Grease hands and shape into balls, doing it as gently as possible. For a different flavor, substitute white sugar for brown sugar and add 1/3 cup cinnamon candies when syrup mixture boils.

Cheese And Eggs

CHEESE AND EGGS

Higgledy, piggledy, my black hen,
She lays eggs for gentlemen.

—*Nursery rhyme*

Back some years ago, no self-respecting Southern house-wife would use cold storage eggs or "shipped in" eggs in her cooking. The eggs had to be absolutely fresh, preferably pro-duced by locally known hens.

To insure a supply of such eggs, many families kept a small flock of chickens back of the house. White Leghorns were favor-ites (they were recommended by county agents as being excel-lent layers), though Rhode Island Reds and Dominiques (usu-ally known as Domineckers) were also popular.

The hen house, in the corner at the back of the lot, had wooden apple crates, their bottoms covered with thick layers of straw, nailed along its inside walls for nests. The roost poles ranged in rows along the back wall, and a latticed door provided entry at the front.

Each nest had in it a nest egg, placed there to show the hen what was expected of her. The finest nest eggs were made of china or glass, but many were simply egg-shaped gourds or dis-carded doorknobs. They served just as well.

The hens, dumb things, did not always lay in the crates provided for them. Some of them stole nests in the high weeds beyond the garden, and, even worse, some chose to lay under-neath the house.

When this happened, it became the duty of the youngest child to crawl under the house, through the powdery gray dust of soil (pocked by doodle-bug holes) that had not been rained upon since the house was built, through the filmy curtains of spider webs, to retrieve the eggs from the stolen nest.

The patterned door at the front of the chicken house supposedly provided an esthetic touch to the structure (honeysuckle was frequently planted to cover the outside walls), but the latticework also provided easy entry for various varmints: 'possums, weasels and such. Raucus, terrified squawkings from the chicken house frequently woke families from slumber, and with sleepy agreement that "something's after the chickens," the male members of the family stumbled out into the dark to investigate.

Usually they were too late: the marauding thief had escaped, and several hens were either dead or missing. The interrupted sleep was less lamented than was the loss of the egg supply.

The supply of fresh eggs was subject to other hazards. A hawk occasionally swooped down on the flock and flew off with a chicken in its claws. However, chicken owners knowledgeable in folkways knew they could keep hawks away by putting a white flint rock in the fireplace where a fire was burning. Other owners of chickens relied more on a gun or a slingshot to rid their premises of hawks.

Then there were the times when the hens just quit laying. This period of non-productivity almost always coincided with the expected arrival of company. It was a terrible plight to be faced with a shortage of eggs just when an abundance was needed to enrich food for guests.

Such ailments as sorehead and pip also took their toll. Children learned early not to throw watermelon rinds where the chickens could peck them: pecking watermelon rinds gave chickens sorehead. Causes of pip were more complex.

In addition to supplying eggs, the chickens furnished feathers for Indians headdresses for games of cowboys and Indians, fertilizer for flower beds, and fat hens (past their prime as layers) for chicken pies and chicken salad.

The chickens served yet another function. On those occasions when adult conversation was considered unfit for young listeners ("Little pitchers have big ears"), the eavesdropping child was banished by being told, "Go feed the chickens."

CHEESE BALL

1 pound sharp Cheddar cheese
1 cup nuts (walnuts or pecans)
6 ounces cream cheese,
  softened
1 tablespoon Worcestershire sauce

1 tablespoon chili powder
¼ teaspoon garlic powder
2 tablespoons instant
  minced onions
Dash Tabasco

Grind cheese and nuts together. Blend in other ingredients and mix well. Shape into ball and chill.

PUFFY CHEESE SANDWICHES (BAKED)

12 slices bread
6 slices cheese
4 beaten eggs

2 2/3 cups milk
½ teaspoon salt
Scattering of paprika

Butter a rectangular baking pan and put six slices of bread in the bottom. Put six slices of cheese (use the natural, not the processed kind) on top of the bread, and cover cheese with the remaining six slices of bread. In other words, put six cheese sandwiches in the bottom of the baking pan. Now beat up the eggs, milk, and salt real well. Pour over sandwiches. Let stand about 45 minutes or an hour. Bake at 325 degrees for an hour. Scoop a bubbly sandwich on to six waiting plates.

SUNDAY MORNING CHEESE GRITS

Cook 1 cup grits according to package directions. When grits (you can start a good argument over whether the word is plural or singular) is done, stir in a cup of rather strong cheese. Cut the cheese into small slivers or shave it thin before adding to hot grits. Stir until cheese melts.

If any grits is left over, pack it in a refrigerator dish and chill it. Slice it, making slices a little less than an inch thick, dip the slices in beaten egg and then in flour. Fry in butter until brown.

CHEESE SOUFFLE

3 tablespoons butter
3 tablespoons flour
1 cup rich milk

½ teaspoon salt
1 cup sharp cheese (grated)
3 eggs, separated

In a saucepan, make a smooth paste of the butter and flour. Gently stir in milk and cook over low heat, stirring all the time, until thick and smooth. Remove from heat. Stir in salt and cheese, mixing until cheese all melts. Set aside to cool. Beat egg yolks and add to mixture. Beat egg whites stiff and carefully fold them in. Spoon into buttered baking dish and bake at 325 degrees about half an hour or until top is brown and puffy. Serve at once.

CHEESE OMELET

2 tablespoons butter or margarine
6 beaten eggs
1/3 cup rich milk

Salt and pepper
1 cup grated sharp cheese

Melt butter or margarine in heavy skillet over low heat. Beat eggs and milk together and season to taste. Pour into skillet. Cook slowly. As eggs begin to set or get firm, lift gently around the edges with a spatula so that uncooked portion can run underneath. When eggs are cooked, sprinkle the top with the grated cheese, fold over, and serve at once.

SUPER-SOUP CHEESE SOUFFLE

1 can condensed cream
  of celery soup
1 cup sharp cheese, grated

6 eggs, separated
Salt and pepper to taste

Put soup (undiluted) and cheese in heavy saucepan and place over low heat until cheese melts. Remove from heat. Beat egg yolks until thick. Stir into soup mixture. Add salt and pepper. Beat egg whites until stiff. Fold soup mixture into beaten whites. Pour into buttered 2-quart casserole. Bake at 325 degrees about 50 minutes or until temptingly brown. Serve at once.

CREAM CHEESE WITH CHIVE OMELET

2 3-ounce packages cream
  cheese, softened
4 teaspoons chives, chopped fine
6 eggs, separated
¼ cup rich milk

1½ teaspoons salt
¼ teaspoon pepper
3 tablespoons cooking oil
Parsley, if desired

Mash cream cheese with fork, add chopped chives, and mix well. Using heavy spoon, beat in egg yolks, one at a time. Blend in milk, salt, and pepper. Beat egg whites until stiff and fold into mixture. Heat cooking oil in large skillet. Pour omelet into skillet and cook over low heat for ten minutes or until bottom is firm and lightly brown (lift up edge and peep). Then bake at 350 degrees for another ten minutes. Remove from oven and loosen around the edges with a spatula. Run the edge of the spatula down the center of the omelet (don't cut all the way through), fold it over carefully, and turn it out on a heated platter. Garnish with parsley, if desired. Serve immediately.

CREAMY SCRAMBLED EGGS

½ to 1 pound bacon
2 tablespoons butter or margarine
8 eggs

½ cup cream
¾ teaspoon salt
Pepper to taste

Cook bacon, drain on absorbent paper and keep warm. Pour off bacon grease. Melt butter in same skillet. Beat eggs. Beat in cream, salt, and pepper. Pour into skillet and cook over low heat, stirring frequently, until thickened but moist. This usually takes about five minutes. Pile creamy eggs onto hot platter and garnish with bacon strips. Serve at once.

RINKTUM DIDDY

1 small onion, chopped
1½ tablespoons butter
1 can tomatoes

Salt and pepper
1 cup cheese cut into small pieces
2 beaten eggs

Saute chopped onion in butter in heavy skillet. Add tomatoes and heat to bubbling. Season to taste. Add cheese and eggs and continue cooking over low heat—stirring, stirring—until cheese has melted and mixture is smooth. Serve on hot buttered buns or toast. This is a fine dish to cook over a campfire since it is virtually foolproof and wonderfully filling.

HARD-BOILED EGGS

Nearly every cook has her own way of cooking hard-boiled eggs and they are not likely to change their methods. So for new cooks here is a suggested procedure:

Put eggs (be sure they are fresh — if they tilt up on end or float in water, they are not) in saucepan and cover with lukewarm water at least an inch and a half over the tops of the eggs. Heat rapidly until water begins to boil. Take pan off stove, cover tightly (do not pour off water!) and let stand for 15 minutes. Pour off the hot water and place the pan with the eggs in it under cold running water. When eggs are cool, hold each one under running water (cold, of course) to peel off the shell.

TRAMP EGGS

Back during the Depression, a tramp stopped to ask for breakfast at a friendly looking house, and he was served fancied-up baked eggs which is what the family happened to be eating that morning. The tramp enjoyed the dish so much that he asked for and got the recipe. From thenceforth the baked eggs became known as Tramp Eggs. Here is how:

Butter a shallow baking dish and carefully break into it the number of eggs required to feed the breakfasters. Pour rich milk around the eggs until the tops of the yolks peep out. Sprinkle with salt and dot with butter. Grate cheese over the top. Bake at 300 degrees until cheese is bubbly and eggs are done to perfection. Serve with hot grits or hot biscuits. Or both.

UNCLE REMUS' ROASTED EGGS

These eggs roast in the hot ashes while stories are being told around a campfire or an open fire. When the stories are over, the eggs are ready. Each listener—and the narrator, too—wraps an egg in four or five thicknesses of newspaper. The paper must be wet. Put the wrapped eggs in the hot ashes and cover them well. When the outer layer of paper is scorched, the egg is done. Roll all the eggs out of the fire, but investigate only one. The others may have to be returned for longer cooking. It takes a little practice to make the stories and the cooking time come out even.

COUSIN LOU'S EGGS AND GREEN ONIONS

12 tender green onions	½ teaspoon salt
2 tablespoons butter	Pinch pepper
¼ cup cream	6 eggs

Chop onions fine (use green tops, too) and saute in butter. Add cream, salt, and pepper to eggs and beat. Combine with onions in skillet and cook over low heat, stirring constantly, until eggs are done.

VEGETABLE EGG BAKE

2 thinly sliced onions	½ teaspoon chili powder
2 chopped green peppers	1 can whole kernel corn,
3½ tablespoons butter	drained
1 cup fresh tomatoes, chopped	2 tablespoons olive oil
1 teaspoon salt	12 eggs
Pepper to taste	

Saute onions and peppers in butter. Add tomatoes, salt, pepper, and chili powder. Cover and cook over low heat for five minutes. Put in shallow, buttered baking dish. Add corn. Sprinkle with olive oil. Break eggs (leave them whole) on top. Season to taste. Bake at 350 degrees about 20 or 25 minutes or until eggs are of desired doneness. Canned tomatoes, well drained, may be substituted for the fresh tomatoes.

MODIFIED EGGS BENEDICT

4 thin slices fried
  Tennessee ham
4 slices toast

4 poached eggs
Hollandaise sauce

Place ham slices on top of toast (ham should be about the size of the toast to look nice, but let it lap over the edges for added goodness) and put a poached egg on top of the ham. Cover with Hollandaise Sauce and serve at once.

Hollandaise Sauce

4 tablespoons butter
2 egg yolks

1½ tablespoons lemon juice
Salt and red pepper to taste

Melt butter in top of double boiler. Remove from stove. Beat egg yolks until it seems impossible that they could need any more beating. Then add a few more licks. Add eggs and lemon juice to melted butter in top of double boiler. Put over hot (not boiling) water and stir until sauce thickens. This should not be more than about two minutes. If sauce cooks too fast, it will curdle. If this happens, do not be too upset; just add another beaten egg yolk. Season with salt and pepper.

HOLIDAY EGGS WITH HAM

6 eggs
1/3 cup rich milk
1 teaspoon salt
Pepper to taste
3 tablespoons butter

1 cup ham scraps,
  finely chopped
¼ cup chopped green pepper
¼ cup diced pimento

Beat eggs and add milk, salt, and pepper. Mix well. Melt butter in heavy skillet. Add ham, pepper, and pimentos and saute for several minutes. Pour in eggs and cook, stirring constantly, until eggs are done. Garnish servings with additional red pimento and green pepper if desired.

EGGS GOLDENROD

3 tablespoons butter
3 tablespoons flour
1 teaspoon salt

Pinch pepper
2 cups milk
8 hard-boiled eggs

Melt butter in heavy skillet over low heat. Stir in flour and seasonings. Pour in milk and stir constantly, being sure to scrape bottom and sides of skillet, until thick and bubbly. Remove from heat. Save two yolks from the eight eggs. Chop the remaining eggs and the two whites coarsely and add to sauce. Stir to mix. Have wedges of crisp toast ready and spoon mixture over them. Garnish with slices from the two egg yolks. This is even better served over slices of hot cornbread.

PICNIC-STYLE STUFFED EGGS

Hard-boiled eggs
Bacon, cooked crisp and
   crumbled or bits of ham,
   cut fine
Paprika, if desired

Mayonnaise
Swish of prepared mustard
Sweet relish
Salt and pepper

Peel hard-boiled eggs and cut them in half. Scoop out the yolks and mix with bacon bits or ham bits, mayonnaise, mustard, relish, and seasonings. Put this tangy mixture back into the whites. Sprinkle on paprika, if desired. Wrap in plastic wrap or waxed paper and take on picnic or dinner-on-the-ground or whatever. This is merely a basic recipe. Imaginative cooks create unforgettable stuffed eggs.

BREAKFAST-WHILE-YOU-DRESS-EGGS

Instant rice
Boiling water

Eggs
Seasoning

Butter muffin pans and put a teaspoon of instant rice in each one. Pour 3 teaspoons boiling water in each one and mix. Now carefully break an egg on top of the rice. Sprinkle with salt and pepper. Place in 350 degree oven and bake about 12 minutes or so or until eggs are of desired doneness. They usually cook just right while the future eaters shower and dress for the day.

HOT EGGS STUFFED WITH HAM

6 hard-boiled eggs
3½ tablespoons sour cream
¼ teaspoon dry mustard
¼ teaspoon salt
Sprinkle of pepper

2/3 cup finely chopped
  cooked ham
1 tablespoon melted butter
Paprika

Cut eggs in half and carefully remove the yolks so that the whites are not marred. Mash yolks with cream, mustard, salt, and pepper. Mix in ham. Refill whites and place in a shallow buttered pan. Brush the tops with melted butter and sprinkle on paprika. Heat in 375 degree oven about 15 minutes. Each heated half may be cut into sections (four is easiest) and speared with a cocktail pick if that is the condition under which they are being served. They are fine eaten with crisp crackers at the kitchen counter, too.

STUFFED EGG CASSEROLE

12 stuffed egg halves
¾ cup rice (raw)
1/3 cup butter or margarine
½ cup minced onions
½ cup minced celery
3 tablespoons flour
3½ cups canned tomatoes

1½ teaspoons sugar
1 teaspoon salt
¼ teaspoon black pepper
¼ teaspoon garlic salt
Buttered bread crumbs, about
  2/3 cup

Cook rice according to directions and spread in the bottom of a buttered casserole dish. Put butter in saucepan and saute onions and celery until tender. Stir in flour, blending well. Add tomatoes and cook until mixture thickens. Stir in seasonings. Pour mixture over rice. Arrange eggs on top. Sprinkle buttered crumbs over the whole thing and bake at 425 degrees about 12 minutes.

STUFFED EGGS WITH SOUR CREAM

6 large eggs, hard-boiled
¼ cup butter, softened
1 teaspoon instant onion
¼ teaspoon salt
Sprinkle paprika
1½ teaspoons mustard
   dressing

8 ounces sour cream
4 tablespoons fine dry
   bread crumbs
½ teaspoon salt
4 tablespoons grated
   Parmesan cheese

Peel eggs and cut each one in half lengthwise. Remove yolks. Mash yolks with butter, onion, salt, paprika, and mustard. Refill egg whites with this mixture. Place stuffed egg halves in buttered oblong baking dish about 10x6x2-inches in size. Spread the sour cream over the eggs so that their tops are covered. Mix bread crumbs (buttered bread crumbs taste elegant), seasoned salt, and grated cheese, and sprinkle this over the sour cream. Bake in preheated 400 degree oven until heated through, about 10 or 15 minutes.

CHEESE WADS

2 cups grated, sharp
   cheddar cheese
1 cup margarine, softened
2 cups sifted flour

½ teaspoon red pepper
1 teaspoon seasoned salt
1 teaspoon Worcestershire sauce

Mix grated cheese and margarine. Work in flour. This can best be done by mixing with hands. Put in pepper, salt, and sauce, mixing well. Then pour in cereal and, using hands, mix without crushing cereal unnecessarily. Shape into small balls (not quite as big as walnuts) and place on ungreased cookie sheets. Flatten each ball with fork. Bake at 375 degrees until balls are light brown, about ten minutes.

Cookies

COOKIES

Hot cross buns!
Hot cross buns!
One a penny, two a penny,
Hot cross buns!

Before there were toll house cookies, there were tea cakes. And before there were tea cakes, there were "little sweet cakes," though

not many Southerners now living can remember the long-ago times when the treats were called by that name.

The very mention of the words "tea cakes" conjures up a rush of happy memories about grandmothers, warm kitchens, the savory goodness of tea cakes eaten with big glasses of rich sweet milk (some families, strangely, preferred buttermilk with their tea cakes, but that was not the norm) to wash the crumbs down, fistfuls of tea cakes taken to treehouses or other childhood hideouts to be shared with playmates or to be eaten in solitary enjoyment, a stack of tea cakes as a surprise in a school lunch pail, tea cakes snapped into small pieces and served on broken china at a dolls' tea party (the dollhouse was laid out among the roots of an ancient oak), and tea cakes providing solace for a childhood hurt or sorrow.

Tea cakes, early on, were tied in clean flour sacks, bleached by many washings, and put on a shelf in the kitchen safe. In grandmothers' houses, the shelf was low enough for children to reach, and the knot was loose enough for children to untie.

Safer storage for the tea cakes was provided by metal lard cans or syrup buckets with tight-fitting lids. Cookie (cooky?) jars came later, probably after the tea cakes themselves became fancier and began taking on different forms and tastes: drop cookies, rolled cookies, bar cookies, refrigerator cookies, and cookies flavored with peanut butter, nuts, raisins, gumdrops, chocolate, lemon, honey, spices, fruits, and such, added singly or in combinations guided only by the cook's imagination.

A generation ago, back during World War II, toll house cookies were the vogue. They were shipped by the millions to servicemen throughout the world, made and mailed by wives and sweethearts and mothers who lovingly hoarded their ration stamps to buy enough sugar to make the cookies.

The recipe for America's most popular cookie was created by Mrs. Ruth Graves Wakefield (she called them Toll House Chocolate Crunch Cookies) at the inn near Boston which she and her husband operated for many years. There is no estimate of the number of such cookies she personally baked before her death in January 1977.

Every family has its favorite cookie recipes. The following are samplings from around the South.

CRISS-CROSS PEANUT BUTTER COOKIES

1 cup margarine
1 cup peanut butter
1 cup sugar
1 cup brown sugar
2 beaten eggs

1½ teaspoons vanilla
2½ cups flour
1 teaspoon baking powder
1 teaspoon soda
½ teaspoon salt

Mix margarine, peanut butter (either chunky or smooth kind may be used), and sugars together well. Add eggs and vanilla and beat. Sift dry ingredients together and sift them into first mixture. Stir to mix well. Shape into 1-inch balls and place these balls about 2 inches apart on ungreased baking sheet. Flatten each ball with the tines of a fork in a criss-cross pattern. It may be necessary to dip fork in flour to keep it from sticking. Bake at 350 degrees until lightly browned.

HERMITS

½ cup butter or margarine
¾ cup brown sugar
2 beaten eggs
1 teaspoon vanilla
1 cup flour

2 teaspoons baking powder
¼ teaspoon salt
1 cup chopped pecans
1 cup finely chopped dates
2 cups bran flakes cereal

Cream butter and sugar. Add eggs and vanilla. Beat well. Sift dry ingredients together and add with nuts, dates, and cereal. Combine well. Drop dabs onto lightly greased baking sheets and bake at 375 degrees about 10 minutes.

COMPANY COOKIES

1 cup butter, softened
1½ cups confectioners'
  sugar, sifted
1 egg

2½ cups sifted flour
1 teaspoon soda
1 teaspoon cream of
  tartar

Cream butter and sugar well. Add egg and beat well. Sift dry ingredients together and add, mixing well. Drop by spoonfuls on ungreased cookie sheet. Bake at 450 degrees about six minutes.

MACAROONS

½ teaspoon salt
3 egg whites
½ cup sugar
¼ teaspoon almond extract
1 teaspoon vanilla
2/3 teaspoon grated lemon
   rind

3 tablespoons sifted cake
   flour
½ cup dates, chopped fine
1 cup ground almonds

Put salt in egg whites and beat until they form soft peaks. Add sugar gradually and beat until a stiff meringue is formed. Add flavorings and grated lemon rind, beating them in. Now fold in flour, dates, and almonds. Gently spoon mixture into small size paper cups. Put the filled cups inside muffin rings for support. Bake at 350 degrees about 15 minutes. Remove cups from muffin rings as soon as taken from oven.

OATMEAL COOKIES

¾ cup butter
1 cup sugar
2 eggs
1 cup (heaping) sifted
   flour
2 teaspoons baking powder
Big pinch salt

1 teaspoon cinnamon
1/3 cup milk
1½ teaspoons vanilla
   (put in milk)
1 cup seedless raisins
3 cups rolled oats

Cream butter and sugar well. Add eggs one at a time, beating after each addition. Combine dry ingredients in sifter and add alternately with milk. Stir in raisins and the oats. Drop by teaspoonfuls onto greased cookie sheet. Do not put too close together. Bake at 350 degrees for 12 to 15 minutes.

LIBERTY BELL MOLASSES COOKIES

1 cup shortening
2 cups brown sugar
1 egg
1 cup molasses
4 cups sifted flour
¼ teaspoon salt

2 teaspoons baking soda
¼ teaspoon cloves
1 teaspoon cinnamon
1½ teaspoons vanilla
½ teaspoon lemon extract
Sugar

Cream shortening and brown sugar well. Beat in egg and molasses, beating until well mixed. Sift remaining ingredients together. Add gradually, beating well. Drop by small spoonfuls onto lightly greased baking sheet. Bake at 350 degrees for 12 to 15 minutes or until lightly brown. Take from oven and sprinkle tops with sugar. Let stand on baking sheet about three minutes before moving to cooling racks.

Cookies will crack on top, like the Liberty Bell.

PLUMP SUGAR COOKIES

1 cup shortening
2 cups sugar
2 eggs, separated
1½ teaspoons vanilla

4 cups sifted flour
1 teaspoon soda
1 teaspoon salt
1 cup buttermilk

Cream shortening and sugar well. Stir in egg yolks and vanilla. Sift dry ingredients together and add alternately with buttermilk. Beat egg whites until stiff and fold in. Drop by tablespoonfuls onto lightly greased cookie sheets. Bake at 375 degrees about 17 minutes.

OATMEAL-MINCEMEAT COOKIES

1¼ cups sifted flour
½ teaspoon salt
¾ teaspoon soda
½ cup shortening

1 cup light brown sugar
1 egg
1½ cups mincemeat
1½ cups quick-cooking oatmeal, raw

Prepare packaged mincemeat according to directions on box, measure out 1½ cups (slightly less will do all right), and set aside. Combine shortening and sugar. Cream well. Add egg and beat until fluffy. Stir in mincemeat. Sift flour, soda, and salt together. Add gradually to creamed mixture, blending well after each addition. Stir in raw oatmeal. Use teaspoon to drop dough onto greased cookie sheet, spacing dabs of dough at least two inches apart. Bake at 350 degrees until brown, about 15 minutes.

GRANDMA'S TEA CAKES

1 cup butter	1 teaspoon vanilla
1 cup sugar	3½ cups flour
3 eggs	

Cream butter and sugar. Add eggs, beating well after each addition. Put in flavoring and add flour to make a stiff dough. Roll thin, cut with big biscuit cutter, and bake at 350 degrees about 10 minutes.

LEMON CRISPS

1 cup butter or margarine	1 teaspoon baking powder
1½ cups sugar	¼ teaspoon salt
1 egg	¼ teaspoon soda
¼ teaspoon vanilla	1/3 cup evaporated milk,
½ teaspoon lemon extract	undiluted
2¼ cups sifted flour	1 tablespoon grated lemon rind

Cream butter with 1 cup of sugar (save other ½ cup) until fluffy. Beat in egg, vanilla, and lemon extract. Sift dry ingredients together and add to butter mixture alternately with milk. Chill about two hours. Roll into balls about the size of bubble gum and then roll balls in mixture of ½ cup sugar and grated lemon rind. Place on baking sheet about 2½ inches apart and cook at 350 degrees for 8 to 10 minutes or until lightly browned. Remove from sheet and cool on wire racks.

FRUITCAKE COOKIES

2½ cups flour
1 pound candied pineapple,
  cut up
1½ pounds candied cherries,
  cut in halves
2½ quarts pecans in
  large pieces
½ pound butter
1 cup sugar

5 eggs
1 small glass sweet
  homemade wine
2 tablespoons dark syrup
½ teaspoon cinnamon
½ teaspoon nutmeg
½ teaspoon allspice
½ teaspoon cloves
Pinch salt

Use ½ cup of flour to coat the fruits and nuts. Stir to coat each piece well. Cream butter and sugar. Add eggs alternately with remaining flour, beating well after each addition. Add wine, syrup, and spices. Combine batter and fruit-nut mixture. Cover and let stand in refrigerator overnight. When ready to bake, drop by spoonfuls on greased cookie sheet and cook at 275 degrees until light brown and firm, about 30 minutes. Remove from cookie sheet immediately but handle carefully as cookies tear when they are hot. Cool on racks and store in airtight containers. These cookies may be frozen. This quantity makes a lot, about two gallons of calorie-filled goodies.

KITCHEN STEP TEA CAKES

1 cup shortening
1 cup sugar
2 beaten eggs
¼ cup milk
2 teaspoons lemon extract or
  orange extract

1 cup cornmeal
3 cups flour
2/3 teaspoon salt
½ teaspoon soda

After creaming sugar and shortening together well, add eggs, milk, and extract. Beat. Gradually add dry ingredients which have been sifted together. Roll thin on lightly floured surface and cut with big biscuit cutter. Bake on greased baking sheet at 375 degrees about 11 minutes. The aroma of the baking cookies should summon hungry children (some adults, too) for a feast of hot tea cakes and cold milk on the kitchen steps.

GUMDROP COOKIES

1 cup shortening
1 cup sugar
1 cup light brown sugar,
   packed
2 eggs
1½ teaspoons vanilla
2 cups flour
1 teaspoon baking powder

1 teaspoon soda
½ teaspoon salt
1 cup shredded coconut
1 cup orange slice candy,
   cut up fine
½ cup chopped nuts
2 cups quick rolled oats

Cream shortening and two sugars. Beat in eggs and vanilla. Sift flour, baking powder, soda, and salt together and add to egg mixture. Stir in coconut, orange slice candy, and nuts. Mix in oats. Shape into balls about the size of the circle on a key chain, place on greased cookie sheet, and press each cookie flat with the tines of a fork. Bake at 350 degrees about 15 minutes. This quantity makes about 60 cookies.

NUTTY COOKIES

1 cup butter or margarine
1½ cups sugar
2 eggs
1 teaspoon vanilla
2½ cups flour
1 teaspoon soda
2 teaspoons cream of tartar

1 small package chocolate
   baking bits
1 cup flaked coconut
1 cup chopped pecans
Mixture of 2 tablespoons sugar,
   2 teaspoons cinnamon, and
   ½ teaspoon nutmeg

Cream butter and sugar. Add eggs, one at a time, beating well after each addition. Stir in vanilla. Sift dry ingredients together and add slowly. Stir in chocolate bits, coconut, and pecans. Form dough into small balls and place on ungreased cookie sheet about two inches apart. Bake at 400 degrees for 10 minutes or until lightly brown. While hot, dust with mixture of sugar, cinnamon, and nutmeg.

GINGERBREAD MEN

8 tablespoons shortening
½ cup sugar
½ cup molasses
1 egg
2 cups flour
½ teaspoon salt

½ teaspoon soda
1 teaspoon baking powder
1 tablespoon ginger
2 teaspoons cloves
2 teaspoons nutmeg
Raisins
Whole cloves

Cream shortening, sugar, and molasses until fluffy. Add egg and mix well. Sift dry ingredients together and add a little bit at a time to creamed mixture. This makes a stiff dough. Wrap in waxed paper and store in refrigerator overnight. Roll out on floured surface and cut with gingerbread man cookie cutter. Decorate cookies with raisins for eyes, nose, and mouth and raisins or whole cloves for buttons. Bake at 350 degrees for ten minutes. Remove from cookie sheet carefully and cool on wire racks. If desired, these men can be "dressed up" with a decorative icing made by melting 1/3 cup shortening in 2 tablespoons milk and blending with 2½ cups confectioners' sugar and a pinch of salt. A drop or two of food coloring will enhance the decorations and will give the slue-footed men a bright-colored suit.

FROSTED CHEWS

¾ cup margarine
½ cup sugar
½ cup brown sugar
½ cup dark corn syrup
1 tablespoon vanilla

4 cups quick oatmeal, uncooked
1 6-ounce package semi-sweet
    chocolate bits
2/3 cup peanut butter (any style)

Cream together margarine and two sugars. Add corn syrup and vanilla. Mix. Stir in oatmeal. Pat dough into bottom of greased 13x9x2-inch baking pan. If dough sticks to hands instead of conforming to pan, moisten fingers a little bit. Bake at 350 degrees for 20 or 25 minutes. Remove from oven and let cool slightly. Put chocolate bits and peanut butter in top of double boiler and melt together over boiling water. Stir constantly. Spread this chocolate-peanut butter topping over the baked layer. Chill to set the chocolate. Cut into bars and serve.

COUNTRY STORE GINGERSNAPS

¾ cup shortening
1 cup brown sugar, packed
1 egg
¼ cup molasses
2¼ cups flour

2 teaspoons soda
1 teaspoon cinnamon
1 teaspoon ginger
½ teaspoon cloves
Dash of salt
Sugar (granulated)

Cream shortening and sugar. Add egg and molasses and cream well. Sift flour with remaining ingredients except sugar and add. Chill dough (covered) an hour or more. Shape into balls and dip the top of each ball in granulated sugar. Place sugared balls sugar side up on greased baking sheet about 3 inches apart. Bake at 375 degrees for 10 or 12 minutes or until just firm. Remove from baking sheet at once.

LONG-REMEMBERED SOFT GINGERBREAD

½ cup butter or margarine,
  softened
¾ cup sugar
1 egg
1 cup molasses
2½ cups sifted flour

1½ teaspoons soda
½ teaspoon salt
1 teaspoon cinnamon
½ teaspoon ginger
¼ teaspoon cloves
1 cup hot water

Cream butter and sugar until fluffy. Add egg and molasses, beating until light. Sift dry ingredients together and add gradually, beating until smooth. Stir in hot water, blending well. Pour into greased 13x9x2-inch pan and bake at 325 degrees about 35 or 40 minutes. Serve warm with lots of butter or with applesauce or with lemon sauce.

CHOCOLATE GRAHAM SQUARES

1 can sweetened condensed milk
2 cups graham cracker crumbs

1 6-ounce package semi-sweet
chocolate pieces

Butter an 11x7-inch pan. Mix ingredients together well and spread in pan. Bake at 350 degrees for 20 minutes. Cool in pan for at least 15 minutes, and then cut into squares. Remove from pan when completely cool. This recipe sounds too simple to be good, but it is fine. The milk must be sweetened condensed, the graham crackers must be crushed into fine crumbs, and the chocolate pieces are dumped in just as they come from the package. Easy. Fine.

BAKED FUDGE SQUARES

2 eggs
1 cup sugar
2 squares chocolate
½ cup milk
½ cup soft wheat flour

¼ teaspoon salt
½ teaspoon vanilla
1 cup broken pecans
1/3 cup melted fat (butter,
   shortening, or oil)

Beat eggs until light and fluffy. Gradually add sugar. Put chocolate in milk and heat over low flame or in double boiler until a smooth, thick paste is formed. Cool thoroughly before adding to egg and sugar mixture. Sift flour and salt into mixture. Then add vanilla and nuts. Fold in melted fat last. Bake in greased 9x9-inch pan at 350 degrees for about 30 or 35 minutes.

When done, cut in squares and dust with powdered sugar.

For some reason this recipe seems to turn out better when it is mixed by hand. If you must use an electric mixer, turn it to the lowest possible speed.

CORNMEAL COCONUT BARS

¾ cup self-rising cornmeal
1 cup light brown sugar, packed
1 cup flaked coconut

2/3 cup finely chopped pecans
2 well-beaten eggs
¼ cup melted butter

Put all dry ingredients together in bowl. Mix eggs with melted butter and add all at once to cornmeal mixture. Stir. Pour into 8-inch square pan which has been lined with waxed paper and greased. Bake at 350 degrees about half an hour. Cool. Remove from pan, peel off paper, and cut into bars.

BLONDE BANANA BROWNIES

1 ripe banana (medium size)
¾ cup sugar
½ cup butter or margarine,
    softened
2 eggs

¾ cup sifted flour
½ teaspoon baking powder
Pinch salt
2/3 cup chopped pecans

Cream banana with sugar and butter until fluffy. Add eggs, mixing well. Sift dry ingredients together and add. Beat until well mixed. Fold in pecans. Pour into (actually spread into is more accurate) greased 8x8-inch baking pan. Bake at 350 degrees for about half an hour. Cool and cut into squares.

ICED TOFFEE SQUARES

¾ cup butter or margarine
4½ cups quick-cooking
    oatmeal, raw
1 cup brown sugar,
    firmly packed
½ cup dark corn syrup

2/3 teaspoon salt
1 tablespoon vanilla
2 cups semi-sweet chocolate
    pieces, melted
1 cup chopped pecans

Melt butter in saucepan (use a big one). Remove from heat and stir in raw oatmeal, brown sugar, corn syrup, salt, and vanilla. Mix well. Pack mixture into well greased 15x10x1-inch jelly roll pan. Bake at 450 degrees about 12 minutes or until brown and bubbly. Cool completely. Loosen around edges and turn out on tray or cookie sheet. Spread with melted chocolate and sprinkle with chopped nuts. Chill in refrigerator. Cut into squares for serving. Keep in refrigerator.

105

GRAHAM CRACKER SQUARES

½ cup brown sugar
½ cup white sugar
½ cup chopped pecans
¾ cup chopped dates

16 graham crackers, crushed fine
2 beaten eggs
1 teaspoon vanilla
Confectioners' sugar

Mix in order given, except for confectioners' sugar. Bake in greased pan about 8x10 inches for half an hour in a 350-degree oven. Cut into squares while hot and roll in confectioners' sugar.

CRISP SUGAR COOKIES

1 cup butter or margarine
1½ cups sifted confectioners'
  sugar
1 egg

1½ teaspoons vanilla
2½ cups sifted flour
1 teaspoon cream of tartar
1 teaspoon soda

Cream butter and sugar. Add egg and vanilla and mix well. Sift dry ingredients together and stir in. Separate dough into two parts, wrap each in waxed paper, and refrigerate at least two hours. Roll thin on floured pastry board, cut into desired shapes, and bake on lightly oiled cookie sheets at 375 degrees until delicately brown. The secret of these crisp cookies is to keep the dough chilled (do not take second package of dough from refrigerator until first is all used) and to handle it as little as possible.

Desserts

DESSERTS

What is sweeter than honey?
—Judges 14:18

Silver-plated cruet stands used to occupy the center of many Southern dining room tables. The stands, usually round with a tall, oval, filigreed handle attached to the center, held salt and pepper shakers with silver-plated tops and clear glass cruets of vinegar and pepper sauce (very hot). Sometimes there was room for a squat mustard jar, also with a silver-plated top, on the stand.

There once was a Southern boarding house, famous for its food, whose owner used the cruet stand to display a daily announcement regarding desserts. A blue ribbon tied to the top of the handle indicated that there would be dessert: cobblers, puddings, pies, cakes, ice cream or such. Absence of a ribbon indicated that boarders should satisfy their longing for a final sweet course by buttering extra biscuits and covering them with ribbon cane syrup, honey, peach marmalade, fig preserves, watermelon-rind preserves, apple butter, crab-apple jelly, blackberry jam, pear conserve, or maybe a sprinkling of plain sugar. Her boarders made do right well even when the cruet stand held no ribbon.

This same boarding house operator used to caution her new diners, "Don't spill anything on my tablecloth. I like a clean cloth. I

change my tablecloth every Saturday. If you spill anything on the cloth, I will expect you to cover the spot with silver coins: dimes, quarters, or half dollars, as needed." She meant it, too. Diners around her table were mighty careful to avoid spills or drips.

About desserts. Good cooks have long known that anyone who learns how to make a perfect boiled custard (rich, thick, creamy-colored, smooth as velvet) can concoct truly elegant desserts quickly and easily.

Plain boiled custard, without any embellishments, is the very favorite dessert of many Southerners. The addition of fruit and/or nuts turns it into something entirely different—and fine! Spooned over slices of cake (a grand way to use stale cake) or over crumbled cookies, used as a sauce on hot gingerbread, chilled and poured over fresh fruit—the possibilities are limitless.

No boiled custard? Then serve ambrosia: orange segments, sugar, grated coconut, and homemade wine. Mix gently, chill, and serve in an elegant glass bowl.

And remember: don't spill anything on the tablecloth!

QUEEN OF PUDDINGS

1 cup crumbled buttered toast	2 cups milk
1 tablespoon melted butter	1 teaspoon vanilla
2 whole eggs	2 egg whites
2 egg yolks	¼ cup sugar
½ cup sugar	Strawberry or cherry preserves

Put crumbled toast in the bottom of a buttered casserole. Spinkle melted butter over crumbs. Combine whole eggs and two egg yolks in bowl and beat slightly. Blend in ½ cup sugar, milk, and vanilla. Pour over toast crumbs. Put casserole in pan of hot water and bake at 350 degrees about 45 minutes or until silver knife inserted in custard comes out clean. Spread preserves over the top of the custard, spreading generously so there will be a thick layer. Make meringue of remaining two egg whites and ¼ cup sugar, beating until stiff peaks are formed. Spread meringue over preserves, sealing it to the edges of the casserole. Bake at 425 degrees about five to eight minutes or until meringue is lightly brown. This fine pudding may be served either hot or cold.

IMPROVED BREAD PUDDING

2½ cups milk	3 cups dry bread crumbs
3 slightly beaten eggs	2 cups thinly sliced
½ cup sugar	pared apples
2 teaspoons vanilla	1 cup raisins

Scald milk. In a medium mixing bowl, combine eggs, sugar, and vanilla. Mix. Gradually pour in the scalded milk, stirring all the while. Butter a 1½ quart casserole and arrange alternate layers of bread crumbs, apples, and raisins in it. Pour on the egg mixture. Let stand half an hour. Occasionally spoon some of the egg mixture from bottom of casserole over the bread on top. Put casserole in shallow baking pan and add hot water to pan in sufficient quantity to come halfway up side of casserole. Bake at 350 degrees until knife inserted in center comes out clean. This should take an hour or more. Let cool ten minutes before serving.

RAISINY RICE PUDDING

2/3 cup seedless raisins
2½ cups half-and-half
2 eggs
Pinch salt
3½ tablespoons sugar

2 teaspoons vanilla
1¼ cups cooked rice
1/3 cup chopped nuts
Whipped topping

Mix raisins in half-and-half and heat slowly. Beat eggs and add salt, sugar, vanilla, and cooked rice. Stir in hot milk (half and half, that is) and raisins. Pour into buttered 1-quart baking dish. Set dish in shallow pan of hot water and bake at 350 degrees for 15 minutes. Sprinkle nuts over top and continue baking for 12 to 15 minutes longer or until custard is barely set in the center. Cool quickly by placing pudding dish in pan of cold water—be careful that sudden change of temperature does not break dish! This quick cooling is supposed to keep the custard creamy. Top with whipped topping at serving time.

BRITTLE APPLE PUDDING

4 cups tart apples
1 cup sugar
½ cup flour

¼ cup butter
1¼ cups crushed peanut brittle

Peel apples and slice them into a buttered casserole. Sprinkle sugar over the apples. A drizzle of lemon juice, though it is not mentioned in the recipe, would not be amiss. Using fingers, mix flour and butter until crumbly. Stir in the crushed peanut brittle. Spread over top of apples. Bake at 425 degrees a little more than half an hour. Serve while still warm.

CITIFIED SWEET POTATO PUDDING

2/3 cup butter
4 cups grated raw sweet
  potatoes
1 cup cane syrup
½ cup sugar
1 cup rich milk

2/3 cup chopped pecans
1 cup raisins
1 teaspoon cinnamon
1 teaspoon allspice
½ teaspoon ground cloves (optional)
2 beaten eggs

Melt butter in heavy iron skillet. Mix well all remaining ingredients except eggs. Add them after everything else is mixed. Pour into hot skillet, stirring a time or two. Put in oven to bake at 350 degrees. When edges crust, turn them under. Do this twice during the approximately 40-minute baking period. Serve hot with a topping of whipped cream.

DELMONICO PUDDING

1 pint milk
3 eggs, separated
1 cup sugar
1 envelope plain gelatin

½ cup cold water
1 teaspoon vanilla
1 dozen almond macaroons

Scald milk in double boiler. Beat the three egg yolks and sugar together. Gradually add to scalded milk. Cook over hot water, stirring constantly, until mixture coats spoon. Soften gelatin in cold water and dissolve in hot custard. Remove from heat. Beat egg whites until stiff and fold them into custard mixture together with vanilla flavoring. Line pudding mold or dainty glass dish with almond macaroons and pour the hot mixture over them. Chill in refrigerator overnight. Top each serving of pudding with a generous dollop of whipped cream and a sprinkle of nutmeg.

GRATED SWEET POTATO PUDDING

3 tablespoons butter or margarine
2 beaten eggs
1 cup brown sugar
½ teaspoon nutmeg

1 teaspoon cinnamon
1 cup rich milk
¾ teaspoon salt
2½ cups grated raw sweet potato

Put butter into heavy iron skillet and place in oven to heat. Cream beaten eggs with sugar. Add other ingredients and mix well. Pour into hot skillet and bake at 350 degrees about 40 minutes. When sides get crusty, scrape and turn crust toward center. Continue baking until browned and firm. Some cooks sprinkle more brown sugar on top just before serving.

FLUFFY COCONUT PUDDING

2 envelopes unflavored gelatin
½ cup cold water
1/3 cup boiling water
6 egg whites
Pinch salt

¾ cup sugar
1 pint heavy cream, whipped
1 teaspoon vanilla
1½ cups coconut, flaked

Sprinkle gelatin in cold water to soften. Add boiling water and stir until dissolved. While this cools, beat egg whites with salt until frothy. Gradually beat in sugar and continue beating until it forms stiff peaks. Beat in cooled gelatin. Fold in whipped cream and vanilla. Butter a deep dish and sprinkle bottom thickly with coconut. Spoon in half of pudding mixture, sprinkle with coconut, add remaining mixture and sprinkle top with rest of coconut. Chill at least four or five hours. Cut into wedges and serve with an apricot sauce or with sweetened fresh berries.

Apricot sauce may be made quickly by combining 1½ cups of apricot jam with ½ cup of water and 4 tablespoons sugar. Simmer over low heat for about ten minutes, stirring nearly all the time.

BOILED CUSTARD

6 egg yolks
Pinch salt

½ cup sugar
4 cups milk
1½ teaspoons vanilla

Beat egg yolks, salt, and sugar together well. Put milk in saucepan and heat to boiling point but do not boil. Pour this hot milk (half of it) a little at a time over the egg yolk mixture, stirring while pouring. Put the remaining milk in the top of a double boiler and pour the egg yolk mixture with the milk added into the top of the boiler, too. Cook over simmering water, stirring slavishly, until custard coats a silver spoon. Remove from heat and stir in vanilla. Occasionally custard curdles. This unhappy condition can sometimes be remedied by beating with a rotary beater.

REAL TREAT EGG CUSTARD

4 beaten egg yolks
¾ cup sugar
2 cups scalded milk
Pinch salt

1 teaspoon vanilla
1 unbaked pastry shell
4 beaten egg whites
½ cup sugar

Beat egg yolks and ¾ cup sugar together until lemon colored. Pour hot (not boiling) milk over egg mixture very slowly, stirring all the time. Add salt and vanilla. Put unbaked pastry shell in oven (400 degrees) about 5 minutes before pouring custard mixture into it. Bake 15 minutes at 400 degrees and then reduce to 250 degrees and bake until pie filling is firm. Make meringue of beaten egg whites and ½ cup sugar and spread over pie. Bake to a golden brown at 300 degrees.

GENTEEL CHARLOTTE RUSSE

1 envelope unflavored gelatin
1/3 cup wine
½ pint cream

3 tablespoons sugar (generous)
½ teaspoon vanilla
3 egg whites

Soften gelatin in wine and then set the cup in container of hot water to heat until gelatin dissolves. Meantime, whip cream and gradually add sugar and vanilla. Beat egg whites stiff and fold into whipped cream. Slowly add wine-gelatin, folding in with respect. Place in refrigerator several hours to set.

LADYLIKE BLANC MANGE

1 envelope unflavored gelatin	1/3 cup sugar
½ cup cold milk	Pinch salt
1½ cups scalded milk	1 teaspoon vanilla

Sprinkle gelatin over cold milk to soften. Add scalding milk (not boiled) and stir until gelatin dissolves. Add sugar and salt, stirring until they dissolve. Add vanilla. Pour into small (½ cup size) molds. Place in refrigerator until firm. Unmold and serve with a brandied cherry sauce.

SYLLABUB

1 cup cream	1 egg white
½ cup powdered sugar	3 tablespoons sherry

Whip the cream with half of the sugar mixed in it. Beat egg white until frothy, gradually add remaining sugar and beat until very stiff. Combine cream with egg, doing it with respect, and slowly add wine. Serve in tall, slender glasses with long silver spoons or pour over fresh fruit in "company" crystal compotes.

MOUNTAINTOP APPLE SNOW

4 egg whites	2 cups applesauce, sweetened and chilled

Beat egg whites until stiff. Gradually and gently fold in the applesauce. Spoon into individual dessert dishes and chill.

HONEY GLAZED BAKED APPLES

6 large, tart, firm apples
6 tablespoons honey
1/3 cup orange juice

Sugar
Nutmeg

Core apples and set them in greased (buttered) baking dish. Mix honey with orange juice and pour into centers of apples. Pour a little hot water in bottom of baking dish. Bake at 400 degrees for about an hour or until apples are tender. Brush tops of apples with additional honey, sprinkle with sugar and nutmeg. Run under broiler to glaze. Serve hot or cold as is, or dress up with whipped cream or ice cream on top.

BAKED APPLE SLICES

8 tart apples
½ cup seedless raisins
  (white preferred)
1 cup orange juice
1/3 cup flour
1/3 cup sugar

½ teaspoon cinnamon
Pinch salt
2 tablespoons grated orange rind
2½ tablespoons butter or margarine
½ cup peanut butter
½ cup chopped salted peanuts

Place thin slices of peeled apples in 2½-quart casserole. Spread raisins over apples and pour on orange juice. Sift dry ingredients together and add orange rind. Combine butter and peanut butter and work into dry ingredients. Spread over mixture in casserole. Sprinkle peanuts on top. Bake at 375 degrees about 45 minutes or until topping is crisp and brown. Apples should be tender by that time, too.

BRANDIED FIGS

2/3 cup sugar
2 cups water
30 dried figs

½ cup cognac
Thick cream

Mix sugar and water in heavy saucepan. Stir over medium heat until sugar dissolves and mixture comes to a full boil. Add figs. Reduce heat, cover and simmer for 15 minutes. Add cognac and continue cooking until figs are plump and soft, about five minutes. Cool. Put into bowl and chill in refrigerator 24 hours or longer. Serve in fancy dishes with thick cream.

BANANA SOUFFLE

2 envelopes plain gelatin	1 teaspoon grated orange rind
½ cup sugar	6 eggs, separated
1/8 teaspoon salt	4 bananas, mashed (about 2 cups)
1½ cups orange juice	1 cup whipping cream

Put gelatin, sugar, salt, orange juice, and orange rind in saucepan, mix well, and bring to a boil while stirring constantly. Remove from heat. Beat egg yolks. Add several spoonfuls of hot mixture to egg yolks, stirring and adding slowly. Pour egg mixture back into pan. Simmer several minutes over low heat. Cool to lukewarm. Stir in mashed bananas. Beat egg whites stiff and fold in. Whip cream (better add two or three tablespoons of powdered sugar to it) and fold it in. Spoon into souffle dish or deep bowl and chill overnight. Serve with rum sauce.

BAKED BANANAS

Roll ripe bananas, peeled, in sugar and cinnamon, allowing one banana per serving. Wrap each banana in rich piecrust pastry rolled very thin. Bake at 450 degrees for 15 minutes. Serve hot with lemon sauce.

UPSIDE-DOWN PEACH GINGERBREAD

1 cup butter
1 cup brown sugar
2 tablespoons light
    corn syrup
2½ cups peach slices
14 pecan halves
½ cup chopped pecans
1 cup sugar
2 cups flour

1½ teaspoons ginger
1 teaspoon nutmeg
1 teaspoon soda
½ teaspoon salt
½ cup molasses
½ cup boiling water
2 eggs
1 teaspoon grated
    lemon rind

Melt ½ cup butter in heavy 10-inch skillet. Add brown sugar and corn syrup, stir over medium heat until blended, and allow to cool. Arrange peach slices on top and dot with pecan halves. Sprinkle with chopped nuts. Cream ½ cup butter with 1 cup sugar until fluffy. Sift flour, ginger, nutmeg, soda, and salt together twice. In a separate bowl, mix molasses and boiling water. Add eggs one at a time to the creamed butter and sugar. Stir in grated lemon rind. Add dry ingredients alternately with molasses mixture. Spread evenly in skillet. Bake at 350 degrees about an hour and a half. Cool a little. Loosen sides with spatula and turn out on platter. Serve hot or cold with whipped cream.

REAL SHORTCAKE

1/3 cup butter
1½ tablespoons sugar
1 egg yolk, beaten
½ cup milk

2 cups sifted flour
2 rounded teaspoons
    baking powder
¼ teaspoon salt
Melted butter

Cream butter and sugar. Add egg yolk and mix well. Pour in milk. Break up butter mixture with spoon so that no big hunks remain. Sift flour, baking powder, and salt together and add to mixture all at once. Mix gently to combine everything. Do not knead. Chill dough.

Roll or pat out on floured surface to ½ inch or more thickness. Cut with big biscuit cutter and place, not touching, on greased baking sheet. Brush tops with melted butter, prick with fork, and bake at 450 degrees about 15 minutes. Split open and serve topped with fresh strawberries or peaches.

FRESH PEACH DUMPLINGS

3 cups sliced fresh
  peaches
2 cups water
1 cup sugar
2 tablespoons lemon
  juice
1 cup pancake mix

1/3 cup brown sugar,
  firmly packed
¼ teaspoon nutmeg
½ cup milk
2 tablespoons butter,
  melted

Put peaches, water, sugar, and lemon juice in big saucepan and bring to boil. Combine remaining ingredients, stirring gently to mix. Drop batter by spoonfuls into boiling peach mixture. Reduce heat and cook, covered (no fair peeking!), for 15 minutes. Serve warm with ice cream.

PEACH MOUSSE

1 envelope plus
  1 teaspoon gelatin
¼ cup cold water
1 8-ounce package cream
  cheese, softened
½ cup sugar
½ teaspoon vanilla

½ teaspoon almond
  flavoring
Pinch salt
1¼ cups milk
1 cup cream, whipped
Sweetened peaches

Soften gelatin in cold water and dissolve over hot water (put cup with softened gelatin in pan of hot water and stir until it dissolves). Combine softened cream cheese, sugar, flavorings, and salt. Beat until smooth. Add milk and gelatin. Chill until partially set. Then fold in whipped cream. Pour into ring mold or into individual molds. Serve with sliced peaches on top. Strawberries may also be used.

OCMULGEE RIVER PEACH COBBLER

3 cups peaches, peeled
and sliced
2½ teaspoons lemon
juice
½ teaspoon almond
extract
½ cup brown sugar

2½ tablespoons butter
1½ cups flour
2 tablespoons white sugar
½ teaspoon baking powder
Pinch salt
1/3 cup salad oil
3 tablespoons milk
Additional sugar and butter

Butter a baking dish and put the peaches in it. Add to them lemon juice, almond extract, brown sugar, and butter. Sift flour, white sugar, baking powder, and salt together. Combine oil and milk and stir the liquid into the dry mixture. Roll dough out and fit it over peaches. Cut "breathing holes" in top and bake at 375 degrees about 40 minutes or until brown. Then sprinkle with sugar and dot with butter and cook 5 minutes more.

CRUSTY PEACH COBBLER

3½ cups sliced fresh
peaches
1/3 cup sugar
1 tablespoon lemon
juice
1 teaspoon grated
lemon rind
1½ cups flour
½ teaspoon salt

3 teaspoons baking powder
1 tablespoon sugar
1/3 cup shortening
½ teaspoon vanilla or
almond flavoring
½ cup milk
1 beaten egg
2 tablespoons sugar
½ teaspoon cinnamon

Spread peaches in bottom of buttered, 8-inch square pan. Sprinkle with sugar, lemon juice, and grated rind. Sift flour, salt, baking powder, and 1 tablespoon sugar together and cut in shortening until mixture is crumbly. Add vanilla or almond flavoring to milk and stir egg into milk. Pour this in all at once on flour mixture and stir just enough to moisten flour. Spread this dough over the peaches. Sprinkle top with 2 tablespoons sugar mixed with ½ teaspoon cinnamon. Bake at 375 degrees for 40 minutes.

CRISP SHORTCAKE

2 cups flour
2/3 cup butter

6 tablespoons confectioners'
sugar

Combine all three ingredients with fork, pastry blender, or fingers until evenly blended. Roll out very thin on floured surface and cut into rounds, 3 inches or so in diameter. Place on baking sheet and cook at 375 degrees until light brown, about 15 minutes. Arrange rounds in layers in serving bowls with sweetened strawberries or peaches between each layer. Top with whipped cream. The pastry does not have to be in symmetrical rounds—it just looks neater that way—so save the leftover scraps with their odd shapes and bake them, too. They will be eaten!

SUMMER DAY FRUIT COBBLER

½ cup butter or margarine
¾ cup flour
2 teaspoons baking
**   powder**
1 cup sugar

Pinch salt
¾ cup milk
2 cups sweetened fruit
**   (berries, peaches,**
**   cherries, etc.)**

Put butter in large baking dish in oven (set oven at 350 degrees) and let it melt while preparing rest of recipe. Sift flour, baking powder, sugar, and salt together and stir in milk. Do not beat, just stir to mix. Pour into baking dish with melted butter. Put sweetened fruit on top of batter. Do not stir. Bake until crusty.

BR'ER RABBIT BLACKBERRY COBBLER

2 cups blackberries,
  sweetened stingily
1 tablespoon flour
  (heaping)
1 cup flour
¼ teaspoon salt

2½ tablespoons butter,
  softened
1/3 cup milk
1 cup sugar
½ cup water

Mix berries with tablespoon of flour and place in deep baking dish. Cover with crust made of flour, salt, butter, and milk. Boil together until sugar is melted, the cup of sugar and the ½ cup water. Pour over crust. Bake at 325 degrees until brown.

STRAWBERRY JOY

2 cups frozen
  strawberries
1 cup whipping
  cream
2 cups crushed
  vanilla wafers

2 tablespoons butter,
  softened
1 cup confectioners' sugar
2 beaten eggs
½ cup chopped pecans

Thaw berries. Whip cream and sweeten to taste. Spread half of vanilla wafers in deep bowl. Cream butter, sugar, and eggs well and spread over wafers. Add layer of nuts, berries, and whipped cream. Top with remaining wafers. Chill in refrigerator.

AGNES SCOTT CRANBERRY CREAM

¼ pound marshmallows,
  cut up
1 can whole cranberry
  sauce
1 cup crushed pineapple

1½ tablespoons lemon
  juice
Pinch salt
1 cup whipping cream,
  whipped

Fold first five ingredients into whipped cream. Chill in freezing unit of refrigerator before serving.

CHOCOLATE SOUFFLE

1/3 cup flour
1/3 cup sugar
3 tablespoons melted
   butter
1 cup light cream

3 well-beaten egg yolks
2 squares unsweetened
   chocolate, melted
1½ teaspoons vanilla
4 egg whites
Sugar

Blend flour and sugar into melted butter. Add cream. Cook over medium-low heat, stirring constantly, until thick. Beat in egg yolks and cook a minute more, stirring hard. Cool a little while. Stir in chocolate and vanilla. Fold in egg whites which have been beaten stiff but not dry. Butter a 1½-quart souffle dish well and coat it with granulated sugar. Carefully spoon mixture into prepared dish. Set dish in pan containing an inch of water and bake at 350 degrees about half an hour or until firm. Serve at once. Top may be sprinkled with confectioners' sugar before serving. Liqueur-flavored whipped cream is perfect atop each serving.

CULTURE CLUB LEMON PIE DESSERT

5 tablespoons
   cornstarch
Pinch salt
1 cup sugar
3 eggs, separated
1 cup boiling
   water

6 tablespoons fresh
   lemon juice
1 tablespoon grated
   lemon rind
1 tablespoon butter
12 ladyfingers
1 cup thick cream,
   whipped

Combine cornstarch, salt, and sugar. Beat egg yolks and add to dry ingredients. Stir in boiling water and add lemon juice, grated rind, and butter. Mix well. Cook over low heat, stirring constantly, until thick and smooth. Beat egg whites stiff and fold in. Pour into mold lined with split ladyfingers. Chill in refrigerator overnight. Serve with whipped cream.

AMBROSIA

Traditionally served at Christmastime, this dessert has only four ingredients: oranges, coconut, sugar, and wine. And the wine may be omitted if necessary. Top quality oranges and freshly grated coconut are preferred. Orange sections, free of peel, pith, and seeds, are cut into dainty bite-size pieces and sprinkled with sugar. Then the grated coconut is mixed in. Proportions vary from kitchen to kitchen, but basically it is about half a cup of grated coconut to four or five oranges with sugar to taste. Pour in the wine (homemade scuppernong or blackberry is fine), mix gently, and let soak up flavors before serving. Some modern-day cooks add cherries, pineapple, and such to the ambrosia, but purists demand the simple goodness of oranges, coconut, sugar, and wine.

FRUITCAKE TRIFLE

2 cups fruitcake, cubed
Bourbon

2 cups applesauce
1 cup boiled custard
1 cup toasted walnuts

After the holidays or after everybody has had all the slices of fruitcake they want, gather up what remains and cut into cubes. Actually the crumbled pieces of the cake do quite nicely. Anyhow, have two cups of the cubes or crumbs, and pour over them as much good bourbon as they can absorb. Let stand an hour or so. While cake is soaking, gently simmer applesauce until it becomes thick. Stir a cup of boiled custard into this applesauce. In a clear glass bowl, arrange a layer of soaked cake, a layer of custardy applesauce, and a scattering of toasted walnuts. Continue until all ingredients are used. All measurements are merely suggestions—this is a sort of use-what-is-available dessert. After the bowl is filled—or the ingredients are all used—chill thoroughly before serving.

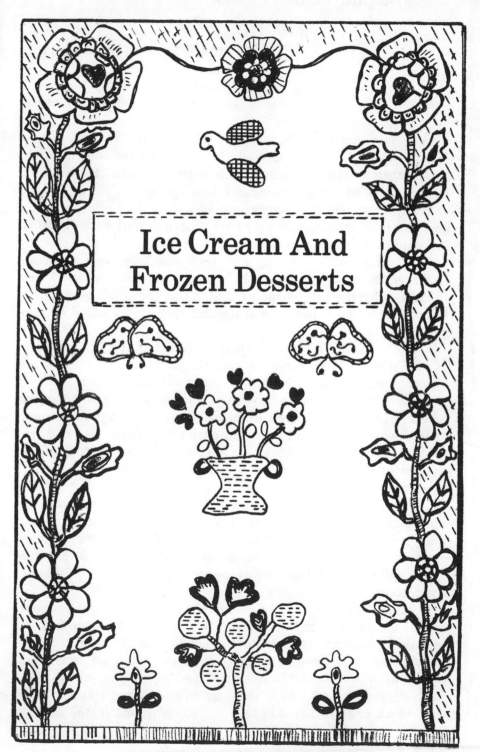

Ice Cream And Frozen Desserts

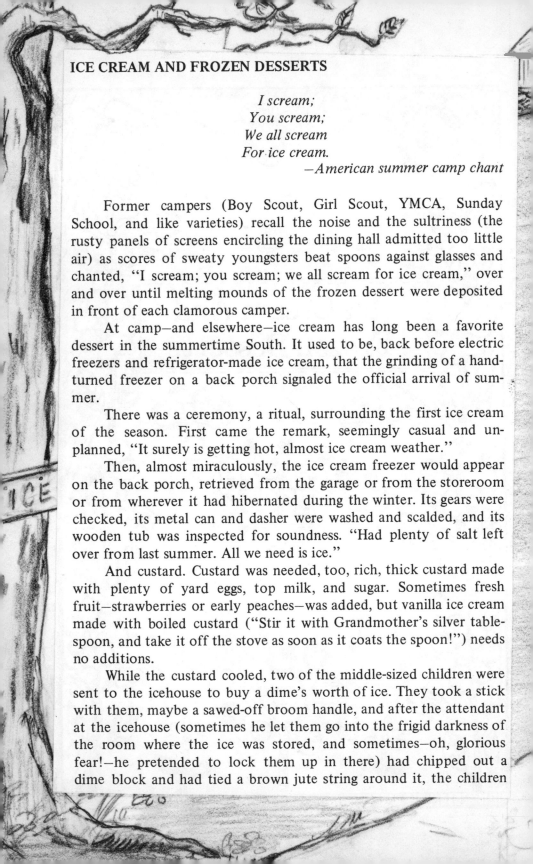

ICE CREAM AND FROZEN DESSERTS

I scream;
You scream;
We all scream
For ice cream.

        —American summer camp chant

Former campers (Boy Scout, Girl Scout, YMCA, Sunday School, and like varieties) recall the noise and the sultriness (the rusty panels of screens encircling the dining hall admitted too little air) as scores of sweaty youngsters beat spoons against glasses and chanted, "I scream; you scream; we all scream for ice cream," over and over until melting mounds of the frozen dessert were deposited in front of each clamorous camper.

At camp—and elsewhere—ice cream has long been a favorite dessert in the summertime South. It used to be, back before electric freezers and refrigerator-made ice cream, that the grinding of a hand-turned freezer on a back porch signaled the official arrival of summer.

There was a ceremony, a ritual, surrounding the first ice cream of the season. First came the remark, seemingly casual and unplanned, "It surely is getting hot, almost ice cream weather."

Then, almost miraculously, the ice cream freezer would appear on the back porch, retrieved from the garage or from the storeroom or from wherever it had hibernated during the winter. Its gears were checked, its metal can and dasher were washed and scalded, and its wooden tub was inspected for soundness. "Had plenty of salt left over from last summer. All we need is ice."

And custard. Custard was needed, too, rich, thick custard made with plenty of yard eggs, top milk, and sugar. Sometimes fresh fruit—strawberries or early peaches—was added, but vanilla ice cream made with boiled custard ("Stir it with Grandmother's silver tablespoon, and take it off the stove as soon as it coats the spoon!") needs no additions.

While the custard cooled, two of the middle-sized children were sent to the icehouse to buy a dime's worth of ice. They took a stick with them, maybe a sawed-off broom handle, and after the attendant at the icehouse (sometimes he let them go into the frigid darkness of the room where the ice was stored, and sometimes—oh, glorious fear!—he pretended to lock them up in there) had chipped out a dime block and had tied a brown jute string around it, the children slipped the stick under the knot and, one holding each end of the stick with the ice between them, they hurried home.

At first, after the ice was shipped and layered with coarse salt around the metal cylinder, everybody wanted to turn the handle, but, toward the last, only the strongest arms could manage the circuit.

With the pronouncement, "It's ready!" the turning stopped. The handle with its gears was removed, briny water was drained from the bunghole ("Don't pour it on my verbena—I'll never get anything to grow there!"), the top was carefully wiped and taken off.

And then the dasher, frozen goodness clinging to its blades, was lifted out and handed to the nearest child.

To be allowed to lick the dasher: memories, not words, preserve that joy.

VANILLA ICE CREAM, CUSTARD KIND

6 tablespoons flour
2½ cups sugar
Pinch salt
6 eggs

½ gallon milk
½ pint whipping cream
1 tablespoon vanilla

Sift flour, sugar, and salt together. Add eggs one at a time, stirring lightly with fork to blend. Scald milk in top of double boiler. Stir in a little hot milk into egg-sugar mixture. Then slowly add egg-sugar mixture to milk in boiler. Cook over hot (not boiling) water, stirring constantly, until custard coats silver spoon. Cool. When cool, add cream and vanilla, and pour into can of gallon freezer. Freeze until firm. Remove dasher *(ready to lick?)*, and dish up ice cream.

SHERRIED MACAROON ICE CREAM

1 cup sherry
1½ dozen almond
    macaroons

1 quart vanilla
    ice cream
¾ cup broken nuts

Pour sherry over crumbled macaroons and let soak for half an hour or so. Soften ice cream so that it can be beaten. When it has been beaten to a creamy but not melted stage, fold in sherried macaroons and nuts. Put in refrigerator trays and freeze until firm.

CHOCOLATE CUSTARD ICE CREAM

2 cups sugar
¼ cup flour
Pinch salt
4 cups milk

4 squares unsweetened
    chocolate, melted
4 beaten eggs
4 cups half-and-half
1 teaspoon vanilla

Sift sugar, flour, and salt into large saucepan. Slowly pour in milk. Cook over medium-low heat, stirring without ceasing, until mixture

128

thickens. Then cook two more minutes. Remove from heat. Stir in chocolate. Put a little hot mixture into beaten eggs. Then put eggs into saucepan. Cook one minute but do not boil. Remove from heat. Add half-and-half and vanilla. Chill thoroughly. Freeze in faithful ice cream freezer. If desired, rum flavoring may be substituted for vanilla. For added goodness, stir in 2 cups miniature marshmallows and 1¼ cups chopped pecans after ice cream is frozen but before it is ripened.

BACK PORCH PEACH ICE CREAM

The sound of the ice cream freezer on back porches once heralded the arrival of summer as surely as protracted meetings and decoration days.

1½ cups sugar	½ pint cream
2 tablespoons flour	2 teaspoons vanilla
¼ teaspoon salt	6 cups mashed peaches
3 beaten eggs	1 cup sugar (to
1 quart milk	sweeten peaches)

Sift sugar, flour, and salt into beaten eggs and mix well. Add milk and cook in top of double boiler until slightly thickened. Add other ingredients and freeze in hand-turned freezer on the back porch.

PEPPERMINT ICE CREAM

1 cup milk	1½ cups whipping cream
16 marshmallows	1 cup peppermint stick
	candy, crushed

Put milk in top of double boiler over boiling water, add marshmallows, and heat until marshmallows melt. Stir often. Chill. Whip cream and fold into marshmallow mixture. Fold in candy. Pour into refrigerator freezing tray and freeze until firm.

BANANA ICE CREAM

2 cups very ripe
  bananas, mashed
1½ tablespoons lemon
  juice
½ cup sugar

2 beaten eggs
Pinch salt
1 cup milk
2 teaspoons vanilla
2 cups heavy cream

Mix ingredients in order given and freeze in hand-cranked freezer until it is hard to turn. This recipe makes about two quarts of ice cream.

FIG ICE CREAM

2 cups sugar
¼ teaspoon salt
2 tablespoons flour
4 cups milk
2 beaten eggs

1 large can evaporated
  milk
4 cups fresh figs,
  peeled and crushed
1 tablespoon vanilla

Sift sugar, salt, and flour together. Add two cups of milk and eggs, mixing well. Cook over low heat, stirring constantly, until thick. Remove from heat. Add remaining two cups of milk and can of evaporated milk. Mix in figs and vanilla. Freeze in hand-turned freezer until firm. May also be frozen in ice trays in refrigerator. If the refrigerator method is used, remove from trays when solid, beat to a smooth texture, and return to trays for freezing until serving time. The old-fashioned ice cream freezer makes better ice cream.

LEMON SHERBET

¾ cup sugar
Dash salt
1 cup water
1 cup half-and-
  half

½ cup fresh lemon
  juice
2 egg whites
¼ cup sugar

Heat sugar, salt, and water in saucepan, bringing to a boil and simmering for five minutes. Cool. Add half-and-half and lemon juice and pour into refrigerator tray. Freeze until firm. Beat egg whites stiff and slowly add ¼ cup sugar. Take frozen mixture from refrigerator, break or cut it into chunks, and beat until smooth. Fold in egg whites and return to freezing tray and refrigerator.

CRUNCHY LEMON DELIGHT

3 eggs, separated
3 large lemons
1 cup sugar

1 large can evaporated
milk, chilled
Vanilla wafers

Beat egg yolks well. Squeeze juice from lemons and combine with sugar. Add to beaten yolks. Whip the evaporated milk and stir it into this mixture. Beat egg whites and fold in. Crush vanilla wafers and sprinkle a thick layer in bottom of refrigerator tray. Pour lemon mixture over crumbs. Sprinkle more crumbs on top. Freeze. Cut in squares to serve.

LEMON MOUSSE

1 cup sugar
¼ teaspoon salt
2 tablespoons
   cornstarch
1 cup milk

3 beaten egg yolks
1/3 cup fresh lemon
   juice
Grated rind one lemon
1 pint cream, whipped

Mix sugar, salt, and cornstarch in top of double boiler. Stir in milk and cook over boiling water about 15 minutes, stirring often. Beat egg yolks in large bowl. When mixture in boiler thickens, pour it slowly over egg yolks, beating all the while. Return to double boiler and cook one minute. Add lemon juice and grated rind. Cool thoroughly. Fold in whipped cream. Pour into refrigerator trays and freeze until firm.

BUTTERMILK SHERBET

4 cups buttermilk
1/3 cup lemon juice
1 cup sugar
1 cup white
  corn syrup

1 cup crushed
  pineapple
4 tablespoons grated
  lemon peel
Pinch salt

Combine all ingredients and mix well. Pour into chilled can of hand-cranked freezer and freeze until firm. Remove dasher *(be sure there is somebody around to lick the dasher—that is part of the tradition!)*, cover freezer with several thicknesses of newspapers or heavy sacks and let sherbet ripen at least an hour before eating.

SHERBET FOR SUNDAY

3 ripe bananas
3 oranges
3 lemons

1½ cups sugar
5 cups milk
½ pint coffee cream

Mash bananas well and add juice of oranges and lemons. Add sugar and stir until dissolved. Mix in milk and cream. Freeze in freezer or pour into freezing trays in refrigerator, freeze to mush, beat until creamy, and return to trays to freeze until hard.

CRANBERRY SHERBET

2 cups jellied
  cranberry sauce
3 tablespoons sugar
1/3 cup orange
  juice

2 tablespoons grated
  lemon peel
2 egg whites,
  stiffly beaten

Use mixer or beater to break up cranberry sauce. Dissolve sugar in orange juice, add lemon peel, and stir into cranberry sauce. Pour into refrigerator tray. Freeze firm. Break into chunks and beat with electric beater until smooth. Fold in egg whites. Return quickly to freezing tray and freeze again until firm.

PINEAPPLE SHERBET

40 marshmallows
2 cups unsweetened
   pineapple juice
1 cup water

4 tablespoons lemon
   juice
5 teaspoons sugar
5 egg whites, beaten
Pinch salt

Heat marshmallows, pineapple juice, and water in double boiler until marshmallows melt. Cool. Add lemon juice and 3 teaspoons sugar. Freeze to mush. Combine beaten egg whites with remaining sugar and salt, fold into semi-frozen mixture, and complete freezing. Serve in chilled sherbet dishes garnished with cherries.

MINCED ICE CREAM PIE

1 cup mincemeat
1 quart vanilla
   ice cream

1 graham cracker
   pie crust
Whipped cream

Follow package directions for preparing mincemeat. Cool. Chill pie crust. Put mincemeat and ice cream in bowl and beat with electric mixer on low speed until two are well combined and of consistency of whipped potatoes. Spoon into pie crust and place in freezer. Slice and garnish each slice with whipped cream when ready to serve.

SINFULLY GOOD DESSERT

3 cups angel food
   cake crumbs
3 pints vanilla
   ice cream
1 small can
   crushed pineapple

1 small package
   frozen strawberries
½ cup chopped pecans
   or almonds
½ cup whipping cream,
   whipped

Break cake into mixing bowl while ice cream softens. Mix cake and ice cream. Now mix in all other ingredients, folding in whipped cream last. Spoon into pan, cover, and freeze.

FROZEN CREAMY PEACH PIE

1½ cups crushed
vanilla wafers
¼ cup melted butter
1 teaspoon lemon
juice
2½ teaspoons orange
juice

½ pound marshmallows,
cut up
1 cup fresh peaches,
crushed
1 cup cream, whipped

Mix vanilla wafer crumbs with melted butter and pat into refrigerator tray to form crust. Put juices in saucepan and heat to boiling. Add marshmallows and melt, stirring as they melt. Cool. Add crushed peaches. Fold in whipped cream. Spoon into wafer-lined ice tray and freeze until firm.

STRAWBERRY SUPREME

1/3 cup butter, melted
2/3 cup flour
¾ cup dark brown sugar
½ cup chopped pecans
2 egg whites

2/3 cup sugar
1½ teaspoons lemon juice
1 16-ounce package frozen
strawberries, thawed
1 cup whipped cream

Melt butter in a shallow pan and add flour, brown sugar, and nuts. Mix well. Bake at 300 degrees for 20 minutes, stirring often. Sprinkle a little more than half of this crumb mixture in a 9x13-inch pan. Beat egg whites stiff and fold in sugar gradually, beating until stiff peaks form. Add lemon juice. Fold in strawberries and whipped cream. Pour over crumbs. Put remaining crumbs on top. Freeze overnight. Serve with strawberries on top.

Meats, Game,
Poultry And Fish

MEATS, GAME, POULTRY AND FISH

Jack Spratt could eat no fat.
His wife could eat no lean.

—Nursery rhyme

Maybe fried chicken is the South's National Dish, but Southerners don't eat it at every meal. Southerners also admire having barbecued ribs, broiled flounder, venison roast, country ham with red-eye gravy, baked chicken and dressing, boiled shrimp, grilled steaks, quail on toast, fried catfish with hush puppies, smothered doves, oyster loaf, souse, roast wild duck, stuffed crab, and pickled pig's feet.

Some Southerners are even partial to chitterlings—but that is an acquired taste that sometimes even borders on being pretentious.

A modern Southern cook knows how to fix ground beef five dozen different ways (a meat loaf made with understanding is fine fare), and she also knows how to cook pork chops with a delicate apricot glaze and to add magical touches to convert plain chicken into a gourmet delight.

More and more Southern cooks, not only those who live near the coast, are featuring fish on their menus as the farm pond, the abundance of fish in local streams and lakes, and the commercial catfish producers make fresh fish constantly available.

The growing popularity of fishing as a sport has almost made it mandatory that cooks learn new and tempting ways to fix fish.

Fishermen know that it's good luck to spit (tobacco juice is highly favored) on the fish hook, and that it is very bad luck to step over a fishing pole, to let two poles cross, or to step on the fishing line.

Although much of the sport fishing is done on the weekends, Southerners—most of them—do know that fishing on Sunday is bad luck, maybe even sinful, but a good many Southern fishermen have gotten over their raising.

OVEN POT ROAST

1½ tablespoons
  cooking oil
4 pound chuck roast
Handful of celery
  leaves
4 carrots, cut up

2 onions, cut up
1 clove garlic, chopped
Fresh ground black
  pepper
Salt to taste
Hot water

Put oil in bottom of heavy iron cooking pot, heat, and brown roast on all sides. Add celery leaves, carrots, onions, and garlic. Sprinkle on black pepper. Stir about ¾ teaspoon salt in a pint of hot water and add. Cover pot and simmer for an hour and a half. Take cover off and add enough water to come up halfway on roast. Put in hot oven (375 degrees) and cook for nearly two hours. Turn roast every 20 minutes so that it will brown properly. If more water is needed, add it. Serve garnished with parsley.

FRUITY POT ROAST

2½-3 pound rump
  roast
3 tablespoons
  shortening
6 potatoes, peeled
  and halved
3 stalks celery,
  cut into pieces

4 carrots, peeled and
  cut into hunks
2 teaspoons salt
½ teaspoon pepper
1 cup dried apricots
1 cup sliced
  mushrooms
1 cup catsup

Brown roast in shortening in Dutch oven. Put vegetables around meat and sprinkle well with salt and pepper. Put apricots and mushrooms on top of meat and pour catsup over the whole thing. Cover and bake at 325 degrees for two and one-half or three hours or until meat and vegetables are tender. Baste occasionally and move roast around to prevent sticking. Taste to see if more salt and pepper are needed.

PIQUANT POT ROAST

3 to 4 pound chuck
  roast
3 tablespoons bacon
  drippings
¼ cup soy sauce
½ cup water
Pepper to taste

1 medium onion,
  sliced
1 small can
  mushrooms
½ cup sliced celery
1 can pineapple
  chunks, drained
¼ cup water
2 tablespoons flour

Brown roast in bacon drippings and pour off excess fat. Add soy sauce, ½ cup water, pepper and onion, cover tightly and cook slowly for 2½ to 3 hours or until meat is tender. Add mushrooms, celery, and pineapple and cook about half an hour longer, until celery is tender. Remove meat to serving platter. Mix ¼ cup water with 2 tablespoons flour. Add to cooking liquid and cook, stirring constantly, until thickened. Serve gravy with pot roast.

SHORT RIB STEW

3 pounds beef
  short ribs
Salt and pepper
2/3 cup flour
4 tablespoons shortening
Boiling water
6 medium potatoes,
  cut in halves

6 large carrots,
  cut in quarters
6 medium onions,
  cut in halves
6 stalks celery,
  cut in quarters

Salt and pepper ribs and coat well with flour. Brown in hot shortening, using heavy skillet or Dutch oven. Add enough boiling water to almost cover ribs. Simmer for an hour. Add potatoes, carrots, and onions, cover, and cook about 20 minutes. Add celery and cook another 15 to 20 minutes. Taste and stir every now and then. Season to taste.

SIMPLIFIED SWISS STEAK

1½ pound shoulder or
  round steak
1 package dehydrated
  onion soup
1 tablespoon margarine
  or butter

1 cup carrots,
  chopped
1 large can mushrooms,
  drained
Tomato wedges

Rub piece of heavy aluminum foil with margarine or butter and put steak in center of it. Sprinkle half of package of onion soup mix over steak, turn it over, and sprinkle rest of onion soup on other side. Dot with 1 tablespoon butter. Put carrots, mushrooms, and tomato wedges on top of steak. Fold foil over the whole thing and seal tightly. Put in a shallow baking pan and bake at 350 degrees for an hour and a half or two hours. The soup mixture usually provides enough salt for this steak, but for salt-fanciers, a shaking of salt should be added before aluminum foil is sealed. As always, the thing to do is to season to taste.

ROUND STEAK BARBECUED IN OVEN

4 slices round steak
Flour, pepper, salt
2/3 cup chopped onion
½ cup celery, diced
3 tablespoons shortening
2 tablespoons brown
  sugar

2 teaspoons prepared
  mustard
2 tablespoons Worcestershire
  sauce
1½ tablespoons vinegar
1 can tomato soup,
  undiluted

Sprinkle steaks with salt and pepper and dredge with flour. Brown onion and celery in shortening in heavy Dutch oven. Brown steaks, add remaining ingredients, cover, and cook at 325 degrees two hours.

MEAT LOAF FOR HUNGRY FAMILY

2 pounds lean
  ground beef
2 slightly beaten eggs
1 cup canned tomatoes,
  drained
1½ cups dry bread
  crumbs

3 tablespoons chopped
  onion
1½ teaspoons salt
2/3 cup nonfat dry
  milk solids

Combine all ingredients in big bowl and mix well. Shape into a loaf (mixture is likely to be sticky so dampen hands for easier handling), place in greased shallow pan, and bake uncovered at 350 degrees about an hour and a half.

MEAT LOAF STUFFED WITH PECANS

2 pounds ground
  round beef
1¼ teaspoons salt
¼ teaspoon pepper

2 tablespoons minced
  onion
1 beaten egg
2 tablespoons evaporated
  milk

Stuffing

2 cups soft bread
  crumbs
1 cup chopped pecans
½ teaspoon salt

3 tablespoons green
  pepper, finely chopped
¼ teaspoon paprika
1 cup milk

Combine six ingredients for meat loaf, mix thoroughly, and pat out into rectangular shape about half an inch thick. Combine stuffing ingredients and spread evenly over meat. Roll up like jelly roll. Place, seam side down, in greased loaf pan and bake at 350 degrees about an hour. Brush top with French dressing when ready to serve.

MINCEMEATED MEATBALLS

2 beaten eggs
½ cup dry bread
  crumbs
1 small can deviled
  ham

1 pound lean
  ground beef
¾ teaspoon salt
Pepper to taste
1 can mince pie filling
½ cup apple juice

Put eggs, bread crumbs, deviled ham, ground beef, and seasonings in large bowl and mix well. Hands may be needed. Shape into small balls, place in shallow baking pan, and bake at 375 degrees until meatballs are done. This should take 15 minutes or so, depending on the size of the balls. Put pie filling and apple juice in pan and heat until bubbly. Add meatballs and stir gently. Serve on beds of hot rice.

CHILI CON CARNE

1 cup onions,
  sliced thin
2/3 cup green
  pepper, diced
4 tablespoons cooking
  oil
1½ pounds ground
  beef

1½ cups boiling
  water
1 20-ounce can tomatoes
2 tablespoons chili
  powder
1½ teaspoons salt
2 cloves garlic, minced
4 cups cooked kidney
  beans

Saute onions and green pepper in oil in heavy casserole or Dutch oven. Add ground beef and cook, stirring constantly, until browned. Add other ingredients except beans, cover, and cook over low heat for an hour. Stir every now and then. Add beans and cook another half hour.

GOURMET GRILLED BURGERS

1½ pounds ground
  beef
1 small onion,
  grated

1½ tablespoons thick
  meat sauce
1 teaspoon salt
¼ teaspoon pepper
¼ pound blue cheese

Season ground beef with onion, meat sauce, salt, and pepper. Shape into 12 patties. Crumble the cheese on top of six of the patties and cover with the other six, sandwich style. Cook over glowing charcoal until the desired stage of doneness is reached.

BEEF ROLL-UPS

1 pound ground
  beef
1½ cups crushed
  cornflakes
1/3 cup chopped onion
1½ teaspoons Worces-
  tershire sauce

1 teaspoon salt
1 teaspoon paprika
Dash pepper
1 8-ounce can tomato
  sauce
8 cabbage leaves
1/3 cup water

Mix well ground beef, cornflake crumbs, onion, Worcestershire sauce, salt, paprika, pepper, and ½ cup of the tomato sauce. Drop cabbage leaves into boiling water and let blanch for three or four minutes. Drain. Divide the meat mixture into eight portions, and put one portion in the center of each cabbage leaf. Fold ends over, roll up, and fasten with toothpick. Place in shallow, buttered baking dish. Mix remaining tomato sauce with water and pour over cabbage rolls. Bake (covered) at 350 degrees for about 45 minutes. Baste occasionally.

GOOD TIMES HOBO STEW

1 pound lean
  hamburger
½ pound frankfurters,
  sliced
1 envelope onion
  gravy mix

1 can tomato sauce
1 can mixed vegetables
1 cup water
Salt and pepper to taste

Brown beef in heavy boiler. Add other ingredients, stir and heat until bubbly. This stew does not have to be eaten beside railroad tracks: it adapts well to any outdoor setting.

SLIGHTLY FANCY CORNED BEEF AND CABBAGE

1 can cream of
  celery soup
½ cup chopped onion
1 teaspoon mustard

1¼ cups canned corned
  beef (or 1 can)
4 cups fresh cabbage,
  coarsely shredded

Combine all ingredients well and place in buttered casserole. Cover and bake at 375 degrees for 45 minutes. It varies somewhat from the kind Jiggs used to crave in the comic strips, but it is a simple recipe.

BAKED SPICY CORNED BEEF

5 pounds (about)
  corned brisket
  of beef
2 tablespoons pickling
  spice
1 orange, sliced
1 onion, sliced

1 stalk celery (leaves,
  too) cut up
1 medium carrot, sliced
1/3 cup brown sugar,
  packed
1 tablespoon prepared
  mustard

Cover corned beef brisket with cold water and soak for an hour. Remove from water and pat dry. Place on large sheet of heavy foil. Pour ½ cup fresh water over top. Sprinkle with spices. Arrange orange slices and vegetables around brisket. Pull foil up and seal with a light double fold. Seal ends and turn up so that liquid will not run out. Place in shallow pan and bake at 300 degrees for 4 hours. Remove from oven, cool slightly, and unwrap. Mix brown sugar with mustard and spread this over meat. Bake uncovered in moderate oven (375 degrees) for about 20 minutes or until brisket is glazed.

CORNED BEEF HASH WITH EGGS

Butter a baking dish about 10x6 inches in size. Pack firmly into it two cans of corned beef hash. Brush top with melted butter. Make nests with the bowl of a large spoon and break an egg into each nest. Season eggs to taste. Bake in oven at 350 degrees until eggs are as firm as desired.

LIVER AND ONIONS

1½ pounds sliced
  beef liver
1½ teaspoons salt
Sprinkling pepper
¼ cup flour
¼ cup bacon
  drippings

1 cup sliced onions
1 cup chopped celery
1 cup green pepper
  slivers
1 can tomatoes
4 cups cooked rice

Season liver slices, coat with flour, and brown in bacon drippings. Remove from skillet. Brown onions in same drippings. Drain off fat (grease) and return liver to skillet with onions. Add celery, pepper, tomatoes, cover and simmer for about 30 minutes or until liver is tender. Serve over hot rice. The celery and green pepper may be omitted, if desired, and traditional cooks did not use tomatoes but added water to simmering liver and onions.

FRENCH-FRIED LIVER STRIPS

1 pound beef liver,
  sliced 1-inch thick
½ cup flour

1 teaspoon salt
¼ teaspoon pepper
Lard for frying

Partially freeze liver slices so that they may be cut easier. Cut the liver into strips about three inches long and half an inch wide. Dredge the strips in flour seasoned with salt and pepper. Fry in deep moderately hot lard (350 degrees) for about three minutes or until lightly browned. Drain on absorbent paper.

BOILED TONGUE WITH BLACKBERRY SAUCE

1 fresh beef tongue
Cold water
1½ tablespoons salt
½ cup diced celery
Flour

1 cup blackberry
  jelly
1 cup raisins (cooked
  soft in 1 cup water)
Juice 1 lemon

Cover tongue with cold water, add salt and celery, and boil gently until tongue is tender. Cool. Remove skin from tongue. Place in a greased baking pan and dust lightly with flour. Combine jelly, raisins, and lemon juice and pour over meat. Bake at 375 degrees about half an hour, basting often with blackberry sauce.

FRUITED PORK CHOPS AND RICE

6 lean pork chops
2½ tablespoons vegetable
  oil
2½ cups chicken broth
  or water
2 teaspoons salt
¼ teaspoon pepper

1 tablespoon soy sauce
1 cup uncooked rice
½ cup seedless raisins
2 tart apples, cored
2 tablespoons sugar
6 tablespoons crushed
  pineapple

Brown pork chops in oil in heavy skillet. Drain off fat. Add broth (or water), seasonings, and soy sauce. Simmer about 15 minutes with skillet covered. Then push pork chops to the side and stir in rice and raisins. When well mixed, put pork chops on top of the rice mixture. Cut each apple into three rings, and put one ring on top of each pork chop. Sprinkle on sugar and fill the rings with crushed pineapple. Cover skillet and simmer 20 minutes or until rice is cooked and liquid absorbed. Fluff rice with fork and serve at once.

PORK CHOPS WITH BROWNED RICE

5 pork chops
1 cup uncooked rice
1 large can tomatoes
½ cup green pepper, chopped

1/3 cup onion, chopped
1½ cups water
Salt to taste
Pepper to taste

Lightly grease deep skillet or Dutch oven and brown the pork chops. Remove when brown. Put rice in skillet and cook, stirring without stopping, until brown. Add remaining ingredients, mix well, and place pork chops on top. Cover skillet and cook over low heat about half an hour or until liquid is absorbed. Turn off heat. Let stand on stove about 20 minutes before serving.

BRAISED PORK BUTT IN CRANBERRY SAUCE

5-pound pork butt
  (fresh or smoked)
1 cup water
¾ teaspoon salt

½ teaspoon pepper
1½ cups whole
  cranberry sauce

Put pork butt in heavy kettle just big enough to hold it. Add water and simmer slowly until water has evaporated—don't let it scorch (the meat, that is). Brown meat in fat left in kettle. Pour off excess fat. Season meat with salt and pepper, add cranberry sauce, cover, and simmer for about 3½ hours or until meat is tender. Peep every now and then to make sure meat is not getting dry. Add a little hot water, ¼ cup at a time, if needed.

APPLES WITH COUNTRY SAUSAGE

4 cups green apples,
  sliced and peeled
2 cups sugar

½ cup butter or margarine
1½ pounds fresh pork
  sausage

Put apples, sugar, and butter in heavy skillet and cook over low heat until sugar melts and apples are glazed well. Stir every now and then. Shape ground sausage into 3-inch patties and, using another skillet, brown these patties over low heat. Cook until done. Serve with glazed apples.

FRIED SALT PORK (POOR MAN'S CHICKEN)

Select pork with a streak of lean in it. Use thick slices and cover with boiling water. Let come to a boil again, remove from heat, and pour off water. Dip slices of meat in cornmeal and fry in hot fat until slices are brown. Drain on paper towel. Allow 3 or 4 slices per serving. Serve with fried green tomatoes and spoonbread or grits.

BAKED HAM SLICE

Thick (1-inch) slice
  uncooked ham
1/3 cup brown sugar
1/8 teaspoon cinnamon
1/8 teaspoon ginger

1/8 teaspoon allspice
2/3 cup canned peach
  juice
2 teaspoons cornstarch
1 tablespoon cold water

Cut fat around edge of ham in several places so ham won't curl up. Rub top of ham with brown sugar. Put in shallow baking dish. Mix spices and stir in a little peach juice to make a smooth paste. Add remaining peach juice to this paste and pour around slice of ham in pan. Bake at 325 degrees for an hour. During the last half hour of baking, baste ham three times with juices in pan. When done, remove ham. Mix cornstarch with water and add to sauce in pan. Stir to mix well. Put pan on top of stove over low heat and cook, stirring constantly, until sauce boils and thickens. Serve sauce with ham.

COUNTRY HAM WITH RED-EYE GRAVY

Take a slice of ham about half an inch thick and make slashes all around the edges in the fat to keep the ham from buckling up while it cooks. Put the ham in a heavy skillet and cook over low heat, turning several times, until brown. Take ham from pan and put it on a platter in a warm place. Add about half a cup of hot water to the drippings in the skillet and cook until the gravy turns red. Have grits and hot biscuits waiting to serve with the ham and gravy.

SKILLET HAM AND CORNBREAD

Cut a slice of ham (½ to ¾ inch thick) in four pieces and brown on both sides in a hot skillet. Make cornbread by a standard recipe (small batch with 1 cup meal or less) and pour the batter over the ham in the skillet. Bake in 400 degree oven for half an hour or until cornbread is brown.

HAM BISCUITS

For family eating, use big, crusty biscuits. Split each one and put in a thick slice of baked or fried ham. For party fare, serve dainty biscuits with thin rounds of ham inside each one.

LATE BREAKFAST HAM AND EGGS

½ cup chopped onion
¼ cup butter or
  margarine
3 tablespoons flour
½ teaspoon salt
Pinch pepper
1 cup coffee cream

1 cup milk
2 cups cooked ham,
  diced
6 hard-boiled eggs,
  diced
½ cup sliced mush-
  rooms (canned)
Hot toast

Saute onion in butter. Add flour, salt, and pepper. Cook over low heat, stirring all the time, to combine well. Slowly add cream and milk. Increase heat a little and cook, with no halt in stirring, until mixture thickens. Turn off heat and add ham, eggs, and mushrooms. Stir. Serve on slices of crisp toast.

EAST TENNESSEE HAM AND SWEET POTATOES

4 slices fully
  cooked ham
4 baked sweet potatoes,
  peeled and mashed
1/3 cup light cream
1 tablespoon honey or
  molasses

2 tablespoons brown
  sugar
1½ teaspoons grated
  orange rind
¼ teaspoon salt
½ cup mincemeat

Put ham slices in bottom of shallow baking dish. Bake at 325 degrees for 15 minutes. While ham is cooking (heating, really), combine all other ingredients except mincemeat. Pile potato mixture on ham slices. Make wells with a large spoon on top of each slice, and fill each well with mincemeat. Return to oven to heat for another 15 minutes.

LAMB STEW

3 pounds lamb shoulder,
  boned and cubed
¾ cup soy sauce
Juice 1 lemon
2 cloves garlic, crushed
2 thick slices salt
  pork, cubed
1 dozen small pearl
  onions
1 bay leaf

¼ teaspoon dry mustard
1 teaspoon chopped
  parsley
1 small package carrots,
  peeled and sliced
8 small potatoes
  (preferably new)
Salt to taste
Sour cream

Marinate lamb in mixture of soy sauce, lemon juice, and garlic for about three hours. Fry salt pork until crisp. Remove crisp pork cubes from skillet and set aside. Brown lamb in pork fat. Add onions, bay leaf, ½ cup of marinade, mustard, and parsley. Simmer slowly for about two hours. Add carrots and potatoes. Cook until tender. Season to taste. Thicken the gravy with sour cream just before serving.

HAM FRITTERS

1 cup sifted flour
1 teaspoon salt
1 teaspoon baking
  powder
2 eggs

¼ cup milk
1 cup ground cooked
  ham
1 tablespoon cooking
  oil
Oil for deep frying

Sift flour, salt, and baking powder into bowl. Beat eggs with milk and stir in ground ham and one tablespoon oil. Combine two mixtures. Stir only enough to mix. Drop from a spoon into deep cooking oil heated to 365 degrees. Fry until brown, three to five minutes. Drain on paper and serve at once. These fritters are good at any meal, and they are a fine way to use up the last bits of ham.

ROAST WILD DUCK

2 wild ducks, dressed   Salt to taste
1 cup soy sauce   2 slices bacon
1 cup lime juice   2/3 cup bourbon

Marinate ducks in mixture of soy sauce and lime juice for several hours. Salt the cavities of the birds (not too much salt!), place them breast sides up in a roasting pan, and put a strip of bacon on each one. Bake uncovered at 450 degrees for half an hour. Remove the bacon strips and reduce the heat to 250 degrees. Pour the marinade and half the bourbon over the ducks. Cover and bake about two hours. During the last hour of roasting, pour the rest of the bourbon over the ducks. Baste with sauce in pan.

Serve with a sauce made this way: Mix juice from can of mandarin oranges (11-ounce size) with 1 teaspoon flour. Cook in saucepan, stirring constantly, until thickened. Skim fat from roasting pan, and add juices that remain to thickened orange juice. Add gradually and stir with dedication to keep sauce smooth. Just before serving, add the mandarin orange sections plus about ½ cup of tart jelly. Heat and ladle over ducks right at serving time.

WILD DUCK, PIONEER STYLE

Parboil dressed duck for about three hours, just simmering gently. Remove from water, dry, cover with clean cloth, and let it rest an hour. While duck rests, make a skillet of old-fashioned corn bread. When bread is cool enough to handle, break it into small pieces, and mix one chopped onion and two stalks of celery, also chopped, with it, using melted butter and broth from the kettle in which the duck was parboiled to moisten. Season stuffing to taste with salt and pepper. An egg may be stirred into this mixture if desired. Stuff duck lightly. Place in roaster and add a can of beef bouillon and 2/3 cup of white wine. If any stuffing was left over, sprinkle it in the roaster or form it into pones and put it in. Cover and bake slowly (275 degrees) about two hours, basting often. Serve at once. Truth is, it tastes best eaten right out of the roaster.

WILD DUCK WITH ORANGES

1 onion	1 teaspoon lemon juice
1 large carrot	Juice 1 orange
1 stalk celery	1½ tablespoons flour
1 duck	2 tablespoons red
1 pint beef stock	currant jelly
Salt and pepper	1 lemon, sliced
	3 oranges, sliced

Slice onion, carrot, and celery in buttered pan and lay dressed duck on top. Add stock, cover and simmer for half an hour. Remove cover and season with salt and pepper. Take duck out of pan and put in oven (using another pan, of course) to brown at 400 degrees. Strain gravy from original pan. Skim off fat. Add lemon juice and orange juice. Mix the flour and jelly together (may have to add a little bit of water to make smooth paste) and add gravy. Simmer until mixture thickens. Drop slices of lemon and oranges in boiling water, drain, and add to sauce (gravy, that is). Pour over browned duck and serve. As an elegant garnish, brown orange slices in butter and dust with brown sugar.

BROILED DOVES

Wash birds thoroughly, split down the back, and wash again. Season all over generously with salt and pepper and sprinkle lightly with flour. Place doves, breast side down, in buttered broiler pan. Put a generous wad of butter on each one of the doves in broiler pan. Brown under broiler on high temperature. When both sides are brown, add a cup of water to pan, and turn broiler heat down to low. Cook for at least an hour, adding water as needed and basting every little bit.

SOUTH GEORGIA QUAIL ON TOAST

Dress small quail, salt and pepper each one, and dust lightly with flour. Brown in butter in heavy skillet. Remove when brown. Put a heaping tablespoon or so of flour in skillet with butter and stir until golden brown. Slowly add water to make a thin gravy. Add ½ cup wine. Return birds to skillet and cook slowly in gravy until tender. Serve on toast or on hot grits. Pour the gravy over the birds and sprinkle with pepper.

SWEET POTATOES STUFFED WITH QUAIL
OR
QUAIL IN YAMS

Simmer giblets from quail until tender in seasoned water. Add 2 or 3 slices of mild onion to water while the giblets simmer. When they are done, mince giblets and onion slices and use to stuff quail. Salt and pepper each bird well. Meanwhile, be baking large sweet potatoes in oven. When potatoes are done, split them, scoop out the centers to make a "nest" for quail, and put a quail in each potato. Dab generously with butter—do not be stingy. Close yams. Bake at 325 or 350 degrees about 50 minutes or until birds are tender.

FRONTIER VENISON ROAST

Venison roast (4 to 6 pounds)	1 tablespoon whole
White vinegar or cooking sherry	black pepper
1 large onion, sliced	Salt to taste

Wash roast well and place in a large bowl. Pour over it equal parts of water and vinegar or sherry, enough to cover it. Add onion and pepper. Let stand, covered, in the refrigerator two or three days. Turn it over several times during this period, if you remember. When ready to cook, remove from marinade, and sear quickly on all sides in hot fat. Salt all sides. Place in heavy pot, add a cup or a cup and a half of the marinade, cover and let it cook slowly, either on low heat on top of stove or in a 325 degree oven for about three hours or until tender. Venison roasts are bad about sticking, so be careful. The safest thing is to put a small rack under the meat. Gravy is made from the drippings in the pot, and old timers liked to add a big handful of crumbled gingersnaps to the gravy for added zest and flavor. If desired, bay leaves, a half dozen or so, and whole cloves, about a dozen, may be added to the mixture in which the venison soaks.

LEG OF VENISON

1 leg of venison, boned
½ cup cooking oil
1½ tablespoons vinegar
1 tablespoon Worcestershire
  sauce
4 tablespoons soy sauce

1 package dehydrated
  onion soup
Salt and pepper
1 onion, sliced
2 garlic buttons, sliced
3 thick slices bacon
2/3 cup sherry

Trim fat from venison. Mix cooking oil, vinegar, Worcestershire sauce, soy sauce, and onion soup well. Let stand about 10 minutes. Salt and pepper venison well and place in foil-lined roasting pan. Place onion slices and garlic slices on top and lay bacon over it all. Pour the mixed ingredients on. Close foil and cover tightly with lid. Bake at 225 degrees eight or nine hours. Remove from oven. Pour in sherry. Let stand one hour.

HILL COUNTRY BRUNSWICK STEW

3 pounds venison, cut
  into small pieces
  and stewed
2 young rabbits, stewed
  and cut into small pieces
  (all bones removed)
4 onions, cut up
8 medium size potatoes,
  cut up

2 cans (No. 2 size) whole
  kernel corn
2 cans tomatoes
1 can okra
2 cans lima beans
½ cup butter
2 quarts liquid in which
  meat was stewed

Combine all in large, heavy pot, add salt and pepper to taste and as many hot red peppers as eaters' insides can tolerate. Cook over low heat about two hours. Stir almost constantly. Invite many friends.

HASENPFEFFER

2 onions
1 lemon
2 tablespoons pickling
  spices

2 rabbits
1 cup vinegar
4 tablespoons butter
Flour

This must be prepared in an earthenware container. Spread a layer of onion slices on the bottom of the crock. Put three thin slices of lemon and 1 teaspoon pickling spices on top of onion. Put a layer of rabbit pieces (rabbits have previously been dressed, disjointed, and cut into serving-size pieces) on top of this. Repeat the layering process until everything is used. End with a layer of onion, lemon, and spices on top. Mix the vinegar with enough cold water to cover the contents of the crock. Pour it in. Then put a plate (not metal!) down in the crock with a weight on top of it to press down on the rabbit and keep the meat in firm contact with the onion and lemon. Let stand at least 48 hours in cool place. Remove rabbit pieces and brown them in butter in heavy skillet. Boil the liquid in the crock (strain it first) for about 10 minutes and add it to the rabbit pieces in the skillet. Simmer slowly until tender. Thicken stock with flour for gravy.

SUNDAY DINNER CHICKEN AND DRESSING

1 large fat hen	8 or 10 cups cornbread,
Salt and pepper	crumbled
Butter	4 slices bread, crumbled
½ cup diced celery	8 hard-boiled eggs, chopped
1 large onion, chopped	Seasonings to taste
2 tablespoons margarine	Broth from chicken

Cover hen with water (the hen is in a large pot, of course, one befitting her size). Add about 2 teaspoons of salt to water and simmer until hen is tender. Do not simmer so long that meat begins to leave bones. Remove from pot and cool. Saute celery and onion in margarine or in chicken fat. Mix with cornbread, bread, eggs, seasonings, and chicken broth to achieve a mushy consistency. Brush hen with butter, sprinkle on salt and put in 375 degree oven to brown. Also put in the oven a greased pan filled with the dressing. Baste hen every now and then. If dressing gets too dry, pour on some chicken broth.

SMOTHERED CHICKEN

Small fryer, cut in half	Juice ½ lemon
½ cup butter	4 tablespoons flour
Salt and pepper	

Rub chicken with butter and sprinkle generously with salt and pepper. Drizzle with lemon juice. Put in shallow, buttered pan and bake at 450 degrees for 30 minutes. Put more butter on, sprinkle with a little flour, cover pan, reduce heat to 300 degrees and cook for about an hour and a half. Baste with butter occasionally.

CHICKEN SOUFFLE

3 tablespoons butter
3 tablespoons flour
1 cup milk
¼ teaspoon salt
2 beaten egg yolks

1½ cups cooked chicken,
  cut in tiny pieces
1 teaspoon onion juice
2 well-beaten egg whites
¼ teaspoon cornstarch
¼ teaspoon sugar

Make cream sauce of butter, flour, milk, and salt. Add egg yolks, chicken and onion juice. Cool. Fold in beaten egg whites to which cornstarch and sugar have been added. Put mixture in buttered casserole, place in pan of hot water and bake at 325 degrees for an hour.

APRICOT CHICKEN

1 frying chicken, cut in
  quarters
Salt and pepper
1 can apricots

¼ cup Worcestershire
  sauce
Juice 1 lemon
1 tablespoon cornstarch

Season chicken with salt and pepper and place in a baking dish with a tight-fitting top. Drain juice from can of apricots and mix with Worcestershire sauce and lemon juice. Pour over chicken. Cover tightly and bake at 350 degrees for 50 minutes. Mix cornstarch with a little water and add to the juice in the bottom of the baking dish. Arrange apricots around chicken, return to oven and bake, un-covered, until gravy thickens and apricots brown slightly, about 10 or 15 minutes.

CHICKEN AND DUMPLINGS

1 3-pound chicken,
  cut up
½ cup butter
1 teaspoon salt
½ teaspoon pepper
4 tablespoons shortening

2 cups flour
2 teaspoons baking powder
1 teaspoon salt
½ cup milk (about)

Place chicken in big pot and cover with water. Heat to simmering stage and add butter, salt, and pepper. Simmer until chicken is tender. Add more water, enough to cover chicken well, and bring to simmering stage again. Drop in dumplings. Dumplings are made by cutting shortening into flour which has been sifted with baking powder and salt and adding enough milk to make a soft dough. Roll out on floured surface until about 1/8 inch thick. Cut into strips about 2 inches long and an inch wide. Now drop these strips into the simmering chicken mixture. Cover tightly and let simmer for 20 minutes. Do not peep!

CHICKEN IN CREAM

1 jar dried beef
3 chicken breasts,
  boned and halved

6 slices bacon
1 can cream of
  mushroom soup
1 pint sour cream

Spread dried beef over bottom of rectangular baking dish. Put layer of chicken breasts on top of beef, arranging them so that they do not overlap. Use two baking dishes if chicken will not fit in one layer. Put a strip of bacon across each breast. Combine the soup and sour cream. Pour over chicken. Bake at 250 degrees for two and one-half to three hours. Serve with a fruit salad for added goodness.

REAL CHICKEN PIE

2½ cups cooked, cut-up
  chicken
Rich pastry for 2-crust pie
6 tablespoons chicken fat
  or butter

6 tablespoons flour
½ teaspoon salt
¼ teaspoon pepper
2 cups chicken broth
1 cup milk

Simmer a chicken, preferably a nice fat hen, in a big pot in boiling (no, not really boiling—simmering), salted water until very done. Cool. Some cooks put onion slices and pieces of celery in the pot with the simmering chicken. When cool, fat will rise to the top. Skim off and save. Also save broth in which chicken was cooked. Remove meat from bones. Some cooks cut this up fine, but do not. It should be in large hunks. Now while the chicken is cooling or soon thereafter, prepare the pastry. Use two-thirds of this pastry to line the bottom and sides of a deep baking dish. The other one-third will be the top crust, so put it aside until needed. Melt the butter in a heavy pan and stir in the flour to make a smooth paste. Add salt and pepper, and slowly pour in liquids, stirring while pouring. Continue to stir while mixture cooks over low heat until thick. Add chicken and pour into the pastry-lined pan. Put the top crust on, pinch the edges together to form a tight seal with the lower crust, and prick this top crust in several places with the tines of a fork to let steam escape. A monogram pricked in the crust would make it mighty fancy. Bake at 425 degrees for 35 minutes or until crust is brown. Occasionally hard-boiled eggs are cut up in this pie (added when the chicken is put in), but the addition of any vegetables is forbidden by traditional cooks.

CHICKEN WITH FRENCH TOAST

½ cup butter or margarine
½ cup flour
1 teaspoon salt
¼ cup chicken broth

1 cup milk
2½ cups cooked chicken,
  diced
8 slices French toast

Melt butter in top of double boiler. Add flour and salt, blending well. Mix chicken broth and milk together, and slowly add this liquid to flour mixture. Cook over hot water, stirring with dedication, until mixture thickens slightly. Add diced chicken and cook ten minutes longer.

Arrange French toast (half of it) in bottom of shallow baking dish. Cover with chicken mixture. Top with remaining half of French toast. Bake at 350 degrees for 15 minutes.

Make the French toast by beating 3 eggs and adding to them 4 teaspoons sugar, ½ teaspoon salt, and 6 tablespoons milk. Dip slices of bread in this mixture, coating each side well. Brown on both sides in butter melted in heavy skillet.

CHICKEN SPAGHETTI

1 hen (about 3½ pounds)
12-ounce package thin
  spaghetti
3 tablespoons margarine
1 onion, chopped
2/3 cup celery, chopped

2 cans cream of
  mushroom soup
1 cup chicken broth
½ cup grated cheese
Ripe olives (optional)
Green olives (optional)
Green pepper (optional)

Simmer hen in salted water to cover until very tender. Cut meat into small chunks. Cook spaghetti (see directions on package), drain, and set aside. Melt margarine in skillet and saute onion and celery in it. This is also the time to saute the chopped green pepper and the chopped olives (about ½ cup of each) if they are to be used. Put cooked spaghetti in deep, buttered casserole. Pour soup and chicken broth over it and mix. Add sauteed ingredients and cut-up chicken. Mix everything well. Taste. If it needs more salt, add it. Sprinkle cheese on top and bake at 350 degrees about 25 minutes or until thoroughly heated. Goes well with hot garlic bread and a tossed green salad.

CHICKEN CREOLE

2 fryers (1½ pounds
  each), cut up
4 tablespoons butter
3 cups cooked ham, diced
2 cloves garlic, sliced
2 cups chopped onion
2 cans stewed tomatoes

1½ teaspoons salt
Several dashes Tabasco
1 large bay leaf
2 cups celery,
  sliced thin
1 cup raw rice
1/3 cup chopped parsley

Wash chicken pieces and pat dry. Melt butter in heavy kettle or Dutch oven and brown ham lightly in it. Saute garlic and onions in this butter also. Add chicken. Add tomatoes, salt, Tabasco, and bay leaf. Cover and simmer for half an hour. Add rice and celery, cover again, and simmer another half hour or until rice is done and chicken is tender. Take bay leaf out. Stir in parsley. Serve at once.

STAY-FOR-CHURCH CHICKEN IN FOIL

1 large fryer, halved
Salt and pepper

1 package dehydrated
  onion soup

Salt chicken lightly and place on large sheet of heavy aluminum foil. Sprinkle with dehydrated soup mixture, being sure that some of the dry soup gets on each piece of chicken. Fold foil tightly around chicken and place on baking sheet. Cook in slow oven (275 degrees) while family goes to Sunday School and stays for church, or about two and one-half hours.

BUTTERMILK FRY

1 fryer-broiler (about
  2½ pounds)
Salt
Pepper

1½ cups buttermilk
Flour
Shortening for frying

Use sharp knife to cut chicken into serving-size pieces. Sprinkle each piece with salt and pepper and then dip into buttermilk. Roll each piece of chicken in flour. Add another sprinkling of salt and pepper. Have shortening about 2 inches deep in heavy skillet, and have it hot. Put chicken in a piece at a time until several pieces are in skillet. Do not crowd. When brown on one side, turn over. Reduce heat and cook for about 15 or 20 minutes. Drain on absorbent paper. Repeat with next batch of pieces. This fried chicken is good hot or cold.

COLOSSAL CALORIES CHICKEN CASSEROLE

2½ cups cooked rice
2 cups cooked chicken,
  cut up
1 cup crushed pineapple
1 cup diced celery
½ cup diced green pepper

1½ cups grated sharp
  cheese
1 cup mayonnaise
¼ cup chopped chutney
2/3 teaspoon salt
Pepper

Mix rice, chicken, pineapple, celery, green pepper, and ¾ cup cheese. Stir in the mayonnaise, chutney, salt, and pepper. Spoon into a buttered two-quart casserole. Sprinkle remaining ¾ cup of cheese on top and bake at 350 degrees for half an hour.

CHICKEN HASH

½ cup chopped onion
½ cup chopped celery
2 tablespoons butter
1½ tablespoons flour

1½ cups chicken broth
2 cups finely chopped
  cooked chicken
Salt and pepper

Saute onion and celery in butter. Add flour and stir until smooth. Slowly add broth. Add chicken and seasonings. Serve in a nest of hot grits.

NEXT DAY CHICKEN CROQUETTES

2 cups cooked chicken,
 cut fine
2 beaten eggs
1 teaspoon lemon juice
¾ cup rich chicken broth,
 or 1 can cream of chicken
 soup

1 tablespoon Worces-
 tershire sauce
1 small onion, grated
1 cup dry bread crumbs
Shortening for frying
Cracker crumbs

Combine everything listed above except shortening and cracker crumbs. Mix well. Cover and chill in refrigerator several hours. Shape into balls about the size of a baby's fist, roll the balls in cracker crumbs, and fry in hot shortening until brown. In preparing this "next day" dish, use sharp scissors to cut the chicken into tiny bits. Cooked turkey may, of course, be substituted for chicken.

CRUSTY CHICKEN LOAF

1 onion, chopped
1 cup celery, diced
4 tablespoons butter
1 loaf bread (regular
 size)

1 hen (4 to 5 pounds),
 cooked and diced
6 eggs, beaten until
 light
1 quart chicken stock
Salt and pepper

Saute onion and celery in butter until tender. Break bread into small pieces. Combine all ingredients and mix well. Bake in large, well-oiled loaf pan (actually two loaf pans will be better) at 350 degrees until a nice brown crust forms on top.

Serve with sauce made by heating together one can cream of mushroom soup, 1/3 cup rich milk, and a dash of black pepper.

SCALLOPED CHICKEN SUPREME

3 tablespoons butter
3 tablespoons flour
2 cups chicken broth
1 cup milk
Salt and pepper ·
3 cups rice, cooked

3 cups cooked chicken,
  diced
1 cup cooked mushrooms,
  sliced
½ cup blanched almonds,
  slivered
Soft bread crumbs

Melt butter in saucepan. Stir in flour to make smooth paste. Add chicken broth and milk, stirring well. Season to taste. Cook, stirring with a will, until slightly thickened. Butter a two-quart casserole. Spread half of rice in bottom of casserole. Put half of chicken over rice, and top this with half of mushrooms and almonds. Pour half of sauce over this. Repeat layers. Pour on the remaining sauce. Sprinkle bread crumbs on top. Bake at 350 degrees for 45 minutes.

BAKED CHICKEN LIVERS WITH RICE

1/3 cup butter
3 tablespoons minced
  onions
2½ cups rice, cooked
½ pound chicken livers

Seasoned flour
1 can cream of chicken
  soup, undiluted
½ cup milk

Melt 1 tablespoon butter in saucepan and saute minced onions in it. Add sauteed onions to rice. Cut chicken livers into one-inch pieces, roll each piece in seasoned flour and brown in skillet, using remaining butter for browning. Combine all ingredients, place in 1½ quart casserole, and bake at 375 degrees until hot and bubbly, about half an hour.

GIBLETS WITH RICE

1 cup brown rice
1 cup chopped celery
1 small onion, chopped
1 clove garlic, minced
1½ teaspoons salt
¼ teaspoon pepper

2 cups boiling chicken
  stock
1 pound chopped
  giblets
Pinch oregano
4 slices bacon,
  partially cooked
Cheese strips

Combine all ingredients except bacon and cheese in 1½ quart casserole. Cover and bake at 350 degrees for 40 minutes. Lift rice with fork to make fluffy. Add bacon, cover, and cook 20 minutes longer. Garnish with strips of cheese before serving.

TANGY ROCK CORNISH HENS

4 Rock Cornish hens
1 teaspoon salt
¼ teaspoon pepper
¼ teaspoon ginger
1 clove garlic, crushed
2 tablespoons lemon juice
4 tablespoons butter,
  softened

4 onions, quartered
4 carrots, sliced
¼ cup giblet stock
1/3 cup frozen orange
  juice concentrate, undiluted
1½ teaspoons soy sauce

Wash hens and pat dry. Place giblets in salted water in saucepan and simmer for stock. Add salt, pepper, ginger, garlic, and lemon juice to butter, and rub this mixture well into the hens. Put hens in roasting pan, and surround them with onions and carrots. Make basting liquid by combining giblet stock, orange juice concentrate, and soy sauce. Roast about an hour in a 350 degree oven, basting every now and then.

OVEN BARBECUED TURKEY

1 small turkey
  (10-12 pounds)
Salt and pepper
2/3 cup catsup
1/3 cup honey

2 tablespoons cooking oil
2 tablespoons vinegar
Dash Tabasco
½ teaspoon smoke-flavored
  salt

Wash and dry turkey. Season with salt and pepper to taste. Make sauce of catsup, honey, cooking oil, vinegar, Tabasco, and smoke-flavored salt. Brush turkey with sauce. Bake at 350 degrees for about three hours or until turkey is tender. Baste with sauce every half hour. If turkey browns too quickly, cover lightly with foil.

HOT TURKEY SOUFFLE

6 slices bread
2 cups cooked turkey,
  diced
2/3 cup chopped celery
½ cup chopped onion
½ cup mayonnaise
¾ teaspoon salt

Pepper to taste
1½ cups milk
3 beaten eggs
1 can cream of mushroom
  soup
½ cup sharp cheese,
  shredded

Grease an eight-inch square baking dish. Cube two slices of bread and put them in the bottom of the dish. Mix together the diced turkey, celery, onion, mayonnaise, salt, and pepper, and put this mixture over the bread crumbs. Cut the remaining four slices of bread into eight triangles and arrange them on top of the turkey conglomeration. Add the milk to the beaten eggs. Pour this over the contents of the baking dish. Cover and chill. Spoon the soup over the top of the casserole and bake at 325 degrees until set, about an hour. Sprinkle cheese over the top about five minutes before taking the dish from the oven.

FRENCH FRIED CATFISH

Cut dressed and skinned fish into slices about one inch thick. Have a deep kettle of fat, deep enough to completely cover the fish, smoking hot and waiting. Salt the fish and dip the pieces in undiluted evaporated milk. Roll in cracker crumbs or in cornmeal and drop into hot fat. When golden brown, drain, and serve hot with melted butter and lemon juice.

STUFFED BAKED SNAPPER

1 large snapper (other baking fish may be used)	½ cup melted butter
Salt and pepper	1/3 cup sherry wine
¼ pound crabmeat	2 beaten eggs
1/3 pound small shrimp	1 cup bread crumbs
1/3 cup chopped onion	1 teaspoon chopped parsley
	2 strips bacon—maybe 3

Split dressed fish in side to form a pocket to hold the stuffing. Salt and pepper fish. Mix together other ingredients except for bacon. Do not use quite all the butter—save a little to pour over the fish. Stuff the prepared pocket. Place fish in shallow buttered pan, pour the remaining melted butter on top, and lay the strips of bacon across the fish. Bake at 375 degrees for about 35 minutes or until fish is done.

BROILED RED SNAPPER

Sprinkle cleaned fish on both sides with salt and pepper. Squeeze on some lemon juice and dot with butter. Place on well-greased broiler pan and broil about three inches from heat for four or five minutes or until fish is brown but not dry. Carefully turn fish over, squeeze on more lemon juice, add more butter, and broil on other side. Fish is done when it flakes easily when tested with fork.

BAKED FILLETS WITH SHRIMP SAUCE

1½ pounds fish fillets	½ teaspoon salt
1/3 cup minced onion	1/3 cup grated Cheddar
1½ cups milk	cheese
3 tablespoons butter or	1 cup cooked shrimp
margarine	2 tablespoons sherry
3 tablespoons flour	1 tablespoon minced parsley
	Dash of pepper

Place fillets in greased baking dish, sprinkle minced onion on them and pour the milk over them. Bake in oven at 400 degrees about 25 minutes. Meantime, melt butter in top of double boiler. Stir in flour, salt, and pepper. When fish is done, take it from the oven and pour the milk into the butter mixture in the boiler. Cook, stirring constantly, until smooth and thick. Stir in cheese until it melts. Add shrimp and sherry. Pour sauce over fish and return to oven for about five or ten minutes or until lightly browned. Sprinkle with pepper and garnish with parsley.

BROILED TROUT

2 to 3 pounds trout	2 tablespoons pickle relish
Salt and pepper	1 tablespoon lemon juice
Butter	¼ teaspoon salt
½ cup mayonnaise	Sprinkle cayenne pepper
	2 egg whites, beaten stiff

Wipe fish with damp cloth and sprinkle with salt and pepper. Place in buttered baking dish. Mix together mayonnaise, relish, lemon juice, salt, and hot pepper. Fold in stiffly beaten egg whites. Set aside. Broil fish two or three inches from heat for about ten minutes or until nearly done. Then spread the sauce over the fish. Return to broiler until sauce is puffy and lightly brown, about two or three minutes. Serve at once.

169

SALMON MOUSSE

2 envelopes unflavored
  gelatin
1 cup cold water
1 cup hot water
Juice ½ lemon
2 cups cooked salmon,
  flaked

1 cup mayonnaise
1 cup cream, whipped
Green pepper strips
Pimento strips

Soften gelatin in cold water. Add hot water and stir until dissolved. Chill until slightly thickened. Squeeze lemon juice over salmon. Add salmon, mayonnaise, and whipped cream to gelatin mixture, folding in gently. Oil a salad mold lightly and line the bottom with alternate strips of green pepper and pimento. Fill with gelatin mixture. Chill until firm.

CREAMED SALMON

1-pound can salmon
Milk
½ cup sliced green
  onions
1 cup celery, thinly
  sliced
½ cup sliced mushrooms
¼ cup butter
5 tablespoons flour

½ teaspoon salt
Sprinkle red pepper
½ cup light cream
1/3 cup sherry
2 tablespoons diced
  pimento
Rice - cooked and hot
1 ripe avocado

Drain liquid from salmon into measuring cup. Fill cup with milk. Saute onions (use green tops, too), celery, and mushrooms in butter until tender but not brown. Stir in flour, salt, and the sprinkle of red pepper. Gradually add milk-salmon liquid mixture, stirring and cooking over medium-low heat until the sauce is thick. Gently stir in cream and sherry. Break salmon into pieces (remove bones, of course) and add with pimento, doing this gently. Serve over hot rice. Garnish each serving with slices of fresh avocado.

SALMON AND CRACKER PIE

1 large can salmon
Milk
1½ tablespoons instant
  minced onion

1 teaspoon salt
Pinch black pepper
1½ cups coarse cracker
  crumbs
3 tablespoons butter

Drain liquid from can of salmon and add enough milk to make 1 cup. Put salmon in bowl and remove bones. Flake. Add other ingredients except cracker crumbs and butter. Mix thoroughly but lightly. Put a layer of cracker crumbs in the bottom of a buttered 9-inch pie plate. Work some of the crumbs up along the sides. Ease the salmon mixture on top of the crumbs. Put little dabs of butter on top. Cover with remaining cracker crumbs. Scatter dabs of remaining butter on the top crumbs. Bake about 15 minutes at 400 degrees.

DEVILED CRAB

1½ tablespoons minced
  onion
3 tablespoons minced
  celery
2 tablespoons butter,
  melted
2 beaten eggs
½ cup coffee cream

1 teaspoon prepared
  mustard
1 teaspoon salt
¼ teaspoon white pepper
Few drops Tabasco
2 cups crabmeat
1 cup crumbs
  (½ cracker, ½ bread)
Butter

Saute onion and celery in melted butter. Remove from heat. Stir in eggs, cream, mustard, seasonings, crabmeat, and half of crumb mixture. Mix well. Fill buttered crab shells or individual baking dishes with mixture. Sprinkle remaining crumbs on top and dot with butter. Bake at 375 degrees for about 20 minutes or until crumbs are brown.

CRAB-BACON ROLLS

1 cup crabmeat	Pinch red pepper
1 egg	1 teaspoon chopped
½ cup tomato juice	parsley
1 cup bread crumbs	½ cup celery, chopped
½ teaspoon salt	fine
Dash black pepper	Bacon

Mix all ingredients, with the exception of the bacon, and form into finger-size rolls. Wrap each roll with a strip of bacon, using toothpicks to hold bacon in place. Place on rack under broiler and cook until bacon is done. Turn very often so that all sides will brown evenly. Serve with tossed green salad and cornbread or hard rolls.

CRAB-FILLED ROLLS

1 1/3 cups crabmeat,	1/3 cup relish
flaked	1 cup applesauce
6 tablespoons celery,	1/3 cup mayonnaise
cut fine	8 hard rolls

Mix first five ingredients well. Split rolls and toast lightly. Spread with crabmeat mixture.

STUFFED CRAB

1½ tablespoons green onion,	¼ cup cream
chopped	1½ cups fresh crabmeat
1½ tablespoons green pepper,	2 tablespoons lemon juice
chopped	1 teaspoon onion juice
1½ tablespoons butter, melted	2 beaten eggs
2/3 cup bread crumbs	¼ teaspoon dry mustard
Seasoned salt	

Saute onion and pepper in butter. Add bread crumbs and cream and cook, stirring, until thick. Remove from heat and add other ingredients. Mixture should be stiff. Pack into baking shells, brush with butter, and cook at 375 degrees until golden brown, about 15 or 20 minutes. This quantity should serve four people.

BAYOU CRAB OMELET

1 cup crabmeat
2/3 teaspoon salt
½ green pepper, chopped
  fine
1 small stalk celery,
  chopped fine

1 small onion, grated
3 eggs, separated
½ teaspoon black pepper
½ teaspoon paprika
Oil for cooking

Mix crabmeat, salt, green pepper, celery, and onion with egg yolks. Beat egg whites until very stiff and pour over other ingredients, mixing slightly after adding black pepper and paprika. Cook in about 1/8 inch of cooking oil in heavy skillet until golden brown on bottom. Fold over or turn omelet completely over (tricky!) so that both sides can brown.

FLOUNDER FILLETS ON ASPARAGUS

1 package frozen
  asparagus
Salt and pepper
3 fresh flounder fillets
¾ teaspoon salt
3 tablespoons flour

¼ cup cooking oil
1/3 cup milk
1 can cream of mushroom
  soup
½ cup sharp cheese,
  grated

Cook asparagus until just tender, season to taste and arrange in buttered glass pie dish. Season and flour fish fillets. Brown quickly on both sides in cooking oil. Drain and place on top of asparagus. Combine milk with undiluted soup to make sauce. Pour this over fish. Sprinkle grated cheese on top. Bake at 350 degrees about 15 minutes until fish is done and cheese is brown and bubbly.

FLOUNDER AU GRATIN

1 large flounder
  (2 to 3 pounds)
Salt to taste
Juice 1 lemon
1/3 cup dry bread crumbs,
  crushed

1/3 cup grated sharp
  cheese
3 tablespoons butter
½ cup onion, minced

Sprinkle dressed fish with salt and lemon juice. Place fish in greased shallow baking dish. Sprinkle with bread crumbs, cheese, bits of butter, and onion. Bake at 375 degrees for about 40 minutes or until fish flakes easily when tested with fork. Baste during baking with juices in pan.

BROILED SHRIMP WITH BARBECUE SAUCE

2 pounds fresh shrimp
1/3 cup chopped green
  onions
1/3 cup salad oil
1 cup chili sauce
1/3 cup lime or lemon
  juice

1½ tablespoons brown
  sugar
½ teaspoon salt
Dash Tabasco
2 teaspoons mustard
2½ tablespoons Worcester-
  shire sauce

Peel and devein shrimp. Saute onion in salad oil until tender but not brown. Add all other ingredients except shrimp. Mix well and simmer, covered, for ten minutes.

Place shrimp in foil-lined broiler pan. Pour sauce over shrimp. Broil, about three inches from heat, for six to eight minutes. Remove shrimp to platter. Pour sauce in separate bowl to serve with the broiled shrimp.

DRIPPY SHRIMP

1 pound butter
5 pounds raw shrimp,
  unshelled
1 bottle Italian dressing

2/3 bottle Worcestershire
  sauce
Juice of 2 lemons
Salt
Pepper

Melt butter in large container, something big enough to hold all the shrimp. A turkey roaster is fine. To the melted butter add all the other ingredients, mixing together well. Bake in 325 degree oven for an hour. Stir every now and then. Lift shrimp out and divide among diners. Pour liquid into individual bowls. Diners peel and dunk their own shrimp. Have plenty of paper napkins!

SHRIMP CASSEROLE

1 can cream of mushroom
  soup
1/3 cup mayonnaise
1/3 cup whole milk
1 pound fresh shrimp,
  boiled and deveined
1 5-ounce can water
  chestnuts, drained and sliced

1 cup celery, diced
2 teaspoons grated onion
2 tablespoons chopped parsley
2 cups cooked rice
Sprinkle of Tabasco
2 cups bread crumbs
4 tablespoons butter,
  melted

Stir together soup (undiluted), mayonnaise, and milk in two-quart casserole. Add shrimp, water chestnuts, celery, onion, parsley, rice, and Tabasco. Mix well. Coat bread crumbs with melted butter and sprinkle over top. Bake at 350 degrees for half an hour.

SHRIMP SPAGHETTI

1 pound fresh shrimp,
  boiled
1 small onion, chopped
2/3 cup celery, diced
4 tablespoons margarine,
  melted
1 teaspoon salt

¼ teaspoon pepper
1 6-ounce can tomato
  paste
1½ cups water
1 8-ounce package
  spaghetti, cooked
Grated Parmesan cheese

Shell and devein shrimp. Cut into two or three pieces, depending on size of shrimp. Saute onion and celery in margarine until tender, using large, heavy skillet with a cover. Add shrimp, seasonings, tomato paste, and water. Cover and simmer gently about an hour. Serve hot over cooked spaghetti. Sprinkle with grated cheese.

SHRIMP CREOLE

4 cups fresh cooked
  tomatoes or canned
  tomatoes, drained
1 cup green pepper,
  finely chopped
1/3 cup celery, chopped
1 bay leaf
Salt and pepper
Cooked rice

Dash red pepper
3 tablespoons chopped
  onion
3 tablespoons butter
1 teaspoon minced
  parsley
1 pound shrimp, boiled
  and cleaned

Put tomatoes, green pepper, celery and bay leaf in heavy vessel and simmer for 20 minutes. Season to taste. Saute onion in butter and add it and parsley to tomato mixture. Add shrimp. Serve over hot, fluffy rice. Purists would demand that at least ½ cup of sliced okra be added to this recipe.

SEAFOOD GUMBO

2 tablespoons bacon
  drippings
2 tablespoons flour
1 onion, chopped
  fairly fine
1 cup cooked ham
  scraps, chopped
2 pounds fresh okra,
  cut up

3 stalks celery, chopped
1 can tomatoes
1 green pepper, chopped
1 pound crabmeat
1 clove garlic, crushed
1½ teaspoons salt
½ teaspoon freshly ground
  pepper
1½ pounds fresh shrimp

Make roux of bacon drippings and flour in Dutch oven or heavy iron pot. Add chopped onion and saute. Add ham, okra, and a little water and cook over medium heat, stirring constantly, about three or four minutes. Pour in two cups hot water. Add everything else except shrimp and cook (simmer) for an hour or more. Stir often and taste every now and then. Throw in anything else gumbo seems to need: bay leaves? thyme? Now add shrimp and cook, still simmering, for 20 minutes. Serve over fluffy rice in big bowls. More water may be added as needed during cooking.

FROG LEGS

Skin and clean frog legs. Drop them into boiling water, right heavily salted, for a few minutes. Then soak them in lemon juice with ice cubes for several hours. Dry well. Dip in beaten egg (some fine cooks prefer heavy cream), roll in seasoned flour, and fry. Drain. Serve at once. They may also be simmered in sherry with a little water added for about 30 minutes.

GLORIFIED SWAMP FROG LEGS

1 cup flour
1/3 teaspoon onion salt
½ teaspoon garlic salt
½ teaspoon celery salt
14 pairs frog legs

2 cups melted butter
2 large cloves garlic,
  chopped fine
½ teaspoon onion salt
½ teaspoon celery salt
Lemon juice

Combine flour with next three ingredients and mix well. Roll frog legs in this mixture until well coated. Combine melted butter with next three ingredients in large skillet. Fry coated frog legs in butter mixture over low heat, keeping pan covered with lid, until legs are golden brown. Squeeze on juice of half a lemon and serve at once. More butter for frying may be needed, depending on size of frog legs.

OYSTERS ROCKEFELLER IN CASSEROLE

1 cup butter
1 onion, chopped fine
1 pint select oysters
1 package frozen chopped
  spinach, thawed
1 bay leaf, crumbled
1 teaspoon salt
¾ cup cracker crumbs

1 teaspoon Worcester-
  shire sauce
2 teaspoons lemon juice
Dash of Tabasco
½ cup grated Parmesan
  cheese
5 slices bacon, cooked
  crisp and crumbled
½ teaspoon grated lemon rind

Melt butter in skillet and saute onion in it. Add oysters and stir them around gently just to heat. Do not cook them. Now add spinach and give it a whirl with the other ingredients. Add bay leaf, salt, cracker crumbs, Worcestershire, lemon juice, and Tabasco. Turn off heat. Mix well but gently. Put into buttered casserole, sprinkle top with cheese, crumbled bacon, and grated lemon rind, and bake at 350 degrees for half an hour.

FRIED OYSTERS

There are two basic rules for frying oysters: (1) Have the grease very hot, and (2) do not crowd oysters. Begin by draining oysters well on paper towels. Season with salt and pepper and roll in cracker crumbs or meal. A big old iron skillet is fine for frying the oysters. Have plenty of hot grease in skillet and fry a few oysters at a time. Your reward will be crisp, delicious oysters.

NOVEMBER NIGHT OYSTER CASSEROLE

2 cups cracker crumbs,
  rolled fine
1 teaspoon salt
1½ teaspoons minced parsley
¼ teaspoon celery salt
½ cup melted butter
1 pint oysters

¼ teaspoon paprika
2 teaspoons chopped
  pimento (optional)
2 beaten eggs
1 cup cream of mushroom
  soup

Add cracker crumbs and seasonings to melted butter. Mix well. Put two-thirds of this mixture in bottom of buttered casserole dish. Combine beaten eggs, undiluted soup, and oysters. Pour this over crumb mixture. Cover oysters with remaining crumb mixture. Bake at 350 degrees for 45 or 50 minutes.

HAM AND OYSTERS

24 to 30 fresh oysters
4 tablespoons butter
4 tablespoons cooking
  sherry

4 large slices hot
  toasted cornbread
4 slices baked Tennessee
  ham
Melted butter

Heat oysters in butter until edges curl, two or three minutes. Add sherry. Stir gently. Put ham on top of hot cornbread squares and put hot oysters on top of ham. Dribble with melted butter.

OYSTER FRITTERS

½ cup milk
1 tablespoon cooking oil
½ cup (generous) flour
2 egg whites

Pinch salt
Sprinkling pepper
12 large oysters
Oil for frying

Mix milk and oil and stir flour into it to make a fritter batter. Stir until smooth. Beat egg whites stiff. Fold egg whites, salt, and pepper into batter. Put drained oysters into batter. Have oil for frying deep and hot but not smoking hot. Dip up a spoonful of batter, making sure it contains an oyster, and drop into the hot fat. Fry several at a time, but do not crowd them. Drain on paper towels and serve at once.

BROILED BON SECOUR OYSTERS

Allow six large, plump oysters per serving. Wipe oysters dry and dip them in melted butter seasoned with salt and pepper. Roll oysters in fine toast crumbs until well coated. Place in broiling pan with narrow-mesh grill and put under broiler, using moderate heat to prevent burning. Brown on both sides. Serve on toast with melted butter, sprigs of parsley, and a slice of lemon.

WINTRY NIGHT OYSTER STEW

5 tablespoons butter
3 dozen oysters
1 teaspoon salt
¼ teaspoon pepper

6 cups rich milk
Paprika
Butter

Heat butter in heavy pan or kettle. Add oysters which have been salted and peppered. Heat gently until edges of oysters begin to curl—a minute or so. Remove from heat. Heat milk until hot but not boiling and combine with oysters. Let reach simmering hot stage but be careful not to boil. Serve in hot soup bowls with a sprinkling of paprika and a dobble of butter.

Pickles, Relishes
And Preserves

PICKLES, RELISHES AND PRESERVES

He hath not deserved the sweet which hath not tasted the sour.
—Richard Taverner (1539)

Peach trees in family orchards used to serve two purposes: they provided fruit for eating, and they provided keen switches for punishing errant children.

Thousands of grown Southerners recall vividly how a peach switch, wielded by a firm parent, nettled and stung bare legs. And when such chastisement was preceded by instructions to the culprit to select and cut the switch to be used in his (or her) punishment, the remembered suffering was doubly acute.

Peach trees, fortunately, had happier associations. There was the goodness of ripe peaches picked from the tree and eaten ("Lean over so the juice won't get on your clothes") on the spot; fresh peach pies and cobblers; freezers of homemade peach ice cream; heaping bowls of sliced peaches in moats of thick cream; tiny monkeys and baskets carved from peach seeds by patient grandfathers.

And then there were peach pickles, peach preserves, peach marmalade, and peach conserve, each prepared according to the rituals of a prized, handed-down family recipe. When the peaches began to ripen, out came the fruit jars, the preserve kettles, the long-handled spoons, the sugar, vinegar, spices—and recipes.

Sometimes family members—sisters, cousins, aunts—gathered to work together in one big kitchen to preserve the fruit. Such gatherings were not always completely harmonious. Bitter arguments could break out over how much spice Grandmother put in her pickles or how long Aunt Mary Lou cooked her fig preserves. ("Nobody could make peach pickles as good as Grandmother's! I remember that she—" "Aunt Mary Lou made the best fig preserves I ever tasted, and she told me—").

Even the vigor and the frequency of stirring the bubbling contents of the kettles—or the advisability of stirring at all—could provoke disagreements. Each of the cooks wanted to

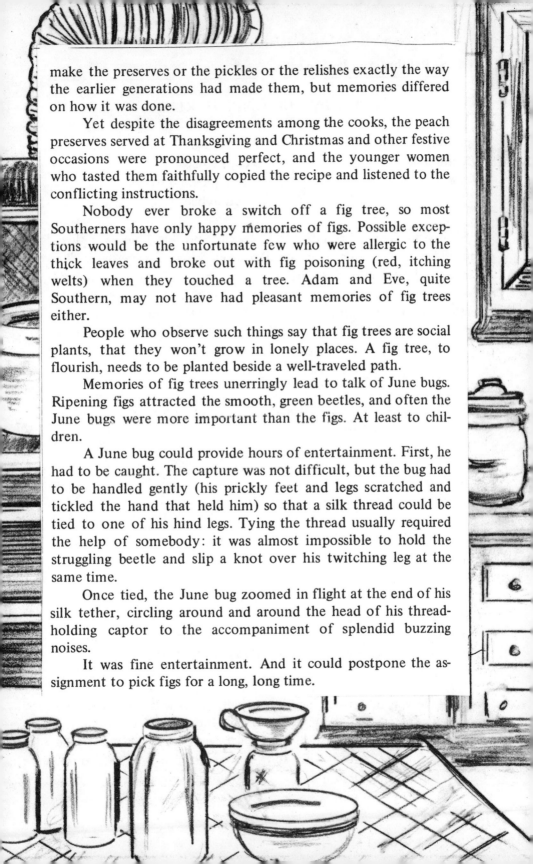

make the preserves or the pickles or the relishes exactly the way the earlier generations had made them, but memories differed on how it was done.

Yet despite the disagreements among the cooks, the peach preserves served at Thanksgiving and Christmas and other festive occasions were pronounced perfect, and the younger women who tasted them faithfully copied the recipe and listened to the conflicting instructions.

Nobody ever broke a switch off a fig tree, so most Southerners have only happy memories of figs. Possible exceptions would be the unfortunate few who were allergic to the thick leaves and broke out with fig poisoning (red, itching welts) when they touched a tree. Adam and Eve, quite Southern, may not have had pleasant memories of fig trees either.

People who observe such things say that fig trees are social plants, that they won't grow in lonely places. A fig tree, to flourish, needs to be planted beside a well-traveled path.

Memories of fig trees unerringly lead to talk of June bugs. Ripening figs attracted the smooth, green beetles, and often the June bugs were more important than the figs. At least to children.

A June bug could provide hours of entertainment. First, he had to be caught. The capture was not difficult, but the bug had to be handled gently (his prickly feet and legs scratched and tickled the hand that held him) so that a silk thread could be tied to one of his hind legs. Tying the thread usually required the help of somebody: it was almost impossible to hold the struggling beetle and slip a knot over his twitching leg at the same time.

Once tied, the June bug zoomed in flight at the end of his silk tether, circling around and around the head of his thread-holding captor to the accompaniment of splendid buzzing noises.

It was fine entertainment. And it could postpone the assignment to pick figs for a long, long time.

CRUNCHY CUCUMBER PICKLES

5 pounds cucumbers	7 cups sugar
2/3 cup lime	5 cups vinegar
Water	½ box pickling spices
	tied in bag

Slice firm cucumbers into stone crock. Sprinkle lime over slices and add enough water to cover. Put crock in cool place overnight. Drain off lime water next morning and soak and rinse cucumbers several times in cold water. Put sugar, vinegar, and spices in large kettle. Stir and heat until sugar dissolves. Add cucumbers and cook until slices are clear. Put into hot jars and cover with syrup. Seal. Process in boiling water for five minutes.

OLD-FASHIONED PICKLE SLICES

4 quarts thinly sliced cucumbers (unpeeled)	Ice cubes
6 medium white onions, sliced	1/3 cup medium coarse salt
1 large green pepper, cut in strips	5 cups sugar
3 cloves garlic, crushed	3 cups white vinegar
	2 tablespoons mustard seed
	1½ teaspoons turmeric

Combine vegetables with garlic and salt, cover with ice cubes, and mix well. Let stand 3 hours or so. Drain thoroughly. Combine the remaining ingredients and pour over the vegetables. Heat just to the boiling point and pour at once into hot sterilized jars. Seal at once. Chill before serving. This quantity makes about eight pints.

SQUASH PICKLES

8 cups tender yellow
squash, sliced
2 cups onions, sliced
Salt

2 cups white vinegar
3 cups sugar
Pickling spices to taste

Combine squash and onion slices in large bowl, sprinkle well with salt, and let stand at least an hour. Drain off liquid which collects in bowl. Put vinegar, sugar, and pickling spices in heavy kettle and bring to full boil. Add drained squash-onion mixture. Bring to boil again. Seal in hot, sterilized jars.

CHOW CHOW

1 head (medium size)
cabbage, chopped
6 onions, chopped
6 green peppers, chopped
6 sweet red peppers,
chopped
1½ pounds green
tomatoes, chopped
1/3 cup salt

1 tablespoon mixed
white pickling spice
2 tablespoons prepared
mustard
1½ quarts vinegar
2½ cups sugar
1½ teaspoons turmeric
½ teaspoon ground
ginger
2 tablespoons mustard seed
1 tablespoon celery seed

Mix vegetables with salt, cover, and let stand overnight. Drain. Put all other ingredients into large kettle (mix prepared mustard with a little vinegar and stir well before adding to mixture in kettle), heat to boiling point, and simmer 20 minutes. Add vegetables and simmer ten minutes. Pack quickly into hot, sterilized jars. Be sure liquid covers vegetables. Seal jars according to directions. Makes about seven pints of chow chow.

GIZRUM

16 large, ripe tomatoes
6 large white onions
6 green peppers
2 cups sugar (heaping)

4 tablespoons salt
1 pint vinegar
Spices to taste
1 red hot pepper
  (if desired)

Put tomatoes, onions, and peppers through the food chopper. Mix all ingredients in big kettle and cook slowly for one hour or longer, until mixture is thick. Stir often to prevent scorching. This gizrum is mighty good served with black-eyed peas or with turnip greens. It is wise to put it in half-pint jars, following the usual directions for sealing, etc., to await the day when extra zest is needed for a meal.

SWEET PICKLED PEACHES

6 pounds peaches
3½ pounds sugar

1 pint vinegar
Cloves

Mix sugar and vinegar in large container, bring to a boil, and boil gently until it boils down to a right heavy syrup. Drop peeled peaches, a few at a time, into the boiling syrup and let them cook until they are tender, about ten minutes. Stick a clove in each peach or add a few cloves to each jar. Place peaches in sterilized jars and pour hot syrup over them to cover. Seal. Clingstone peaches are best for making sweet pickles.

EGGPLANT RELISH

1 quart ground eggplant
1 quart ground cabbage
1 quart white onions,
  ground
5½ tablespoons salt

1 quart apple cider
  vinegar
2 cups sugar
2½ tablespoons celery seed
4½ tablespoons dry mustard
2 hot red peppers

Mix vegetables in large crock, cover with salt, and let stand overnight in cool place. Next morning drain liquid from vegetables. Put them in large kettle and add vinegar, sugar, and spices. Stir hard. Cook over medium heat until mixture boils. Let simmer for half an hour, stirring often, pack in hot jars, and seal.

WATERMELON RIND PICKLES

3 quarts prepared
  watermelon rind
¾ cup plain salt
  (not iodized)
3 quarts cold water
3 trays ice cubes

1 tablespoon whole cloves
5 sticks cinnamon
  (1-inch size)
9½ cups sugar
3 cups white vinegar
3 cups water
2 lemons, thinly sliced

Choose watermelons with thick, firm, unblemished rinds. Cut rinds into sections for easier handling. Peel the green outer covering from the sections and also cut off the pink edges. Cut into cubes. Mix salt with cold water in crock or churn. Put in prepared rind. Add ice cubes and let stand for about 6 hours. Drain. Rinse well. Put rind in large pan, cover with water, and cook for about 10 minutes or until tender when stuck with fork. Drain. Tie spices in thin white cloth. Put sugar, vinegar, and water in large pan with spice bag. Stir to help sugar dissolve. Boil for 5 minutes and then pour over rind. Put in lemon slices. Cover and let stand overnight.

Next morning put rind and syrup (lemon slices, too) in large container and cook until cubes of rind are transparent. Actually they're more translucent. Anyhow, this should take about 10 or 12 minutes. Pack in hot, clean jars and pour boiling syrup into each jar, filling to about ½ inch of top. Put on lids. Jars are then to be processed in boiling water, enough to cover jars, for five minutes. Let jars cool on wire rack.

CRISP PICKLED GREEN BEANS

2 pounds whole beans
  (small)
¼ teaspoon per pint jar
  hot red pepper, crushed
½ teaspoon per pint jar
  whole mustard seed

½ teaspoon per pint jar
  dill seed
1 clove garlic per
  pint jar
5 cups vinegar
5 cups water
½ cup salt

Wash beans. Drain. Cut into lengths to fit neatly into pint jars. Pack beans in hot jars. Add pepper, mustard seed, dill seed, and garlic to each jar. Combine vinegar, water, and salt in large saucepan and heat to boiling. Pour boiling liquid over beans, covering them, and filling jars to within ½ inch of top. Adjust jar lids as required and process in boiling water for five minutes.

PEAR RELISH

4 quarts pears, cored
  and peeled
8 bell peppers
2 red hot peppers
2 quarts onions
12 dill pickles

2 cups salt
4 tablespoons dry mustard
2 teaspoons turmeric
8 tablespoons flour
4 cups brown sugar
2 quarts vinegar

Put pears, peppers, onions, and pickles through food chopper. Sprinkle salt over the mixture and let stand overnight. Next day sift together mustard, turmeric, flour, and sugar. Heat vinegar and make smooth paste of dry mixture. Boil five minutes, stirring constantly. Drain pear mixture and squeeze out juice. Add to boiling liquid, heat thoroughly and place in sterilized jars.

HOT PEPPER JELLY

3 bell peppers, ground
  (1 cup)
6 hot peppers, ground
  (½ cup)
6½ cups sugar

1½ cups apple cider vinegar
1 6-ounce bottle
  liquid pectin
7 or 8 drops food coloring

Combine ground peppers, sugar, and vinegar and boil until peppers are tender—two or three minutes. Strain. Bring liquid to a rolling boil, add pectin and food coloring (either red or green), and boil one minute. Pour into hot sterilized jelly glasses and seal. Makes about seven one-half pints. *This jelly looks bland—but it is not!*

CITRUS-CRANBERRY RELISH

1 cup fresh cranberries
1 orange

1 apple
2/3 cup sugar

Remove stems from cranberries and wash. Drain. Cut orange into quarters and remove seeds. Cut apple into quarters and remove core but do not peel. Put fruits through food chopper, mix well, and stir in sugar. Chill in covered container overnight to blend flavors.

CORN RELISH

18 ears fresh corn
5 onions (medium),
  chopped
2 red peppers
3 green peppers
1 large cabbage, chopped
2 bunches celery, chopped

9 bell peppers, chopped
4 tablespoons dry mustard
3 boxes brown sugar
  (1 pound each)
½ cup salt
2 quarts vinegar
2 tablespoons turmeric

Cut kernels from ears of corn. Mix with other ingredients and cook in large container, stirring often, until green peppers turn brown. Seal in clean, hot, waiting jars.

JERUSALEM ARTICHOKE RELISH

2 pounds Jerusalem
  artichokes
4 yellow onions
3 red peppers
1 cup salt

1 quart cider vinegar
2 cups sugar
1 tablespoon mustard seed
1 tablespoon celery seed

Use a stiff brush to scrub artichokes well. Chop coarsely. Chop onions and peppers coarsely. Put chopped vegetables and salt in large bowl and cover with cold water. Put in refrigerator overnight, being sure to cover it tightly. Next day, pour off the water and place vegetables in large kettle. Add other ingredients and cook over moderate heat, stirring, until sugar is completely dissolved and mixture boils. Reduce heat and simmer for half an hour or until relish is thick. Stir right often during the simmering. Ladle into sterilized pint or half-pint jars and seal. This makes about four pints.

GREEN TOMATO RELISH

1 peck green tomatoes,
  ground
1 cup salt
1 head cabbage (medium)
6 green peppers
5 red peppers

6 medium onions
3 quarts white vinegar
8 cups sugar
2 tablespoons celery seed
2 tablespoons mustard seed
1 tablespoon whole cloves

Mix green tomatoes and salt and place in cloth bag to drain overnight. Grind cabbage, peppers, and onions together and mix with tomatoes in large kettle. Add other ingredients, bring to a boil, and cook until onions are tender, about 20 minutes. Seal in hot, sterilized jars. Makes 10 to 12 pints.

FIG CONSERVE

2 pounds fresh figs
3 cups sugar

1 large orange (juice
  and grated rind)
2/3 cup chopped pecans

Wash figs well, remove stems, and cut into small pieces. Put in pan with sugar, grated orange rind, and juice from orange. Heat slowly, stirring, until sugar melts. Cook until mixture is thick and translúcent, about 50 minutes. Stir often to prevent sticking. Add pecans. just before cooking time ends. Pack in sterilized jars. This conserve is a delicious topping for desserts as well as being a prized taste treat with hot buttered biscuits.

GENUINE FIG PRESERVES

4 quarts ripe figs
5 pounds sugar

2 lemons, sliced

Select ripe but firm figs. Wash well. Finicky cooks soak figs in lime water, and some cooks even peel them, but this isn't necessary. It is also easier to leave the stems on the figs: they make good handles for lifting a sweet morsel onto a buttered biscuit—or into an open mouth. To make the preserves, cover the bottom of a large enamel boiler (white, of course) with a layer of sugar. Put a layer of figs on top of this. Alternate the layers until the figs and sugar are used up, ending with a layer of sugar. Be sure all figs are covered with sugar. Put a top on the boiler and put it in the refrigerator overnight. Next morning cook on low heat until the sugar is all melted. Then increase the heat until a rolling boil results and syrup begins to thicken. Put the lemon slices in. Decrease the heat and cook, stirring every now and then to prevent burning, until figs are clear and syrup is thick. Let figs stand in syrup for several hours, even overnight, to make them plump. Bring to boiling point again, put in pint jars (be sure some lemon slices get in each jar) and seal.

FIG MARMALADE

3 pounds ripe figs   2 pounds sugar
4 oranges

Cut figs into small pieces. Remove seeds from oranges and run oranges through food chopper. Combine figs, oranges, and sugar and cook, stirring almost constantly, until mixture is thick and jellylike, about an hour or more. Spoon into small jars and seal.

STRAWBERRY PRESERVES

4 cups firm strawberries   4 thin lemon slices
4 cups sugar

Wash, hull, and drain berries. Layer berries, sugar, and lemon slices in heavy utensil and let stand about two hours. Heat slowly to rolling boil. Skim off scum, but stir berries as little as possible. Boil for 15 or 20 minutes. Juice will congeal and drip very slowly off spoon when berries are done. Let stand overnight to plump berries. Reheat and pour into sterilized jars. Seal with paraffin.

BLACKBERRY JAM

Wash berries well so that all dust and sticks are removed. Drain. Put in kettle and cook until berries are soft. Do not add water for this cooking—the water that clings to the berries after they are washed and drained will be enough. Put cooked berries through a colander. For each cup of pulp add (but not right now) 1½ cups sugar. Bring pulp to rolling boil. Add sugar, stirring it in slowly. Bring to boil again and let boil, stirring constantly, for one minute. Pour into jars and seal.

MUSCADINE JAM

Wash purple muscadines and remove stems. Pop the pulps out of the hulls and chop the skins. Boil the hulls (skins) in enough water to prevent sticking until tender, about 20 minutes. In another container, boil the pulps with a little water. When pulps are soft, press through a colander to remove seeds. Mix seeded pulps and hulls. Measure mixture, and add ¾ cup sugar for each cup of muscadines. Bring slowly to a boil and simmer until mixture is thick. Seal in hot jars.

ROSY PEAR PINE PRESERVES

3 pounds pears
1 tablespoon grated
　orange rind
6 tablespoons lemon juice
1 cup diced pineapple
　(drained)

5½ cups sugar
1/3 cup maraschino cherries,
　halves
6 drops red food
　coloring

Peel, halve, and core pears. Cut in strips and cut strips into half-inch wedges. Combine all ingredients except cherries and food coloring in large kettle and bring to rolling boil. Boil until thick, about 20 minutes. Stir to prevent sticking or scorching. Add cherries and food coloring and remove from heat. Skim. Pour into hot, sterilized jars and seal at once. This makes about 3 pints.

PEAR CHIPS

8 pounds pears
5 pounds sugar
¼ pound ginger root,
　thinly sliced

2 lemons
1 cup water
½ cup vinegar

Peel and core pears and slice in thin, quarter-inch slices. Combine with sugar and let stand overnight. Next morning add ginger root and lemons cut in very thin slices. Add water and vinegar and cook slowly, stirring often, until thick. Seal in hot jars.

PURE PEACH PRESERVES

Select firm but ripe peaches. Peel and slice. Weigh or measure slices and add 2/3 as much sugar as there is fruit. Cover sliced peaches with the sugar and let stand for several hours, maybe even overnight. Gently bring the sugar and peaches to a boil, and cook until mixture is thick and clear. If peaches are very ripe, add about two teaspoons of lemon juice for every cup of fruit, making this addition during the last few minutes of cooking. A quarter of a teaspoon of salt for every four pounds of fruit will also add to the flavor. Seal in sterilized jars.

BRANDIED FRUIT

2 cups apples, peeled and sliced

2 cups pears, peeled and sliced

2 cups peaches, peeled and sliced

2 cups fresh pineapple, diced

2 cups white seedless raisins

5 cups sugar

5 cups light brown sugar

1 quart good brandy

1 stick cinnamon (if desired)

Prepare fruits and place in large bowl with sugars. Cover bowl and let stand at least an hour. Every now and then gently move fruits around (use fingers) so that they are coated with sugar. Be careful not to crush fruits. Pack into a large stone crock (1½ gallon size) or into several large-mouth quart containers with tight lids. Fill the container or containers with brandy, and add cinnamon stick, if desired. Seal tightly and put away for six months before using.

Pies

PIES

Sing a song of sixpence,
A pocket full of rye,
Four and twenty blackbirds
Baked into a pie.

Although most Southerners are familiar with the poetic pie that was set before the king, an informal—but authentic—survey in the Deep South states has failed to find anyone who has ever eaten a blackbird pie.

Deep South pie fanciers favor other kinds of pies: peach, chess,

black bottom, strawberry, potato, cherry, vinegar, lime, dewberry, apple, lemon, pecan, and such. Rhubarb pies are almost as rare in the South as are blackbird pies.

Most pie-eaters know that it is proper to save the pointed tip of the wedge of pie for the last bite. According to an old superstition, a wish will come true if the top of the pie is cut off, pushed to the side of the plate, and eaten last. The wish must be repeated (silently) just before this last bite is taken, and not a word must be spoken until everyone has left the table.

Southern cooks take pride in their pies, and whether it is a plain chess pie or a fancy gelatin concoction of several layers with a whipped cream topping, they strive for "high company quality."

Nowhere are finer pies found than at dinners-on-the-ground at country churches, churches with names like Bethel and Shiloh and New Fellowship and Oak Grove. Years ago, families used to bring dinner to those church homecomings in trunks, putting the pies (many different kinds) in the tray of the trunk so that the meringue, standing three inches high or more, would not get mashed. Sometimes the fruit pies would be stacked one on top of another like thin layer cakes. Those pies weren't sliced stingy either: everybody got generous portions, plenty of plump points to wish on.

Pies have been little involved in literature. Why have they inspired almost no poetry except for the nursery rhymes about the blackbirds and about Little Jack Horner? There is one story, however, about a boy and pies that has endured for many years. The boy was named Epaminondas, and his story was written by Sara Cone Bryant back in 1907.

Poor Epaminondas couldn't do anything right. When his mammy warned him, "You mind how you step in those pies set out on the steps to cool," Epaminondas minded by carefully stepping right in the center of each one!

These pies whose recipes are given on the following pages are not to be stepped in—and remember to save the points to wish on with the last bite.

STANDARD PIE CRUST

2 cups flour
½ teaspoon salt

2/3 cup shortening
6 tablespoons cold water
(ice water)

Put flour and salt in large mixing bowl. Cut in shortening until mixture looks like coarse meal. Sprinkle cold water evenly on the surface and stir with a fork until the dry particles are moist. Form into a ball, and divide this ball into two parts. Roll each half into a 12-inch circle. Fit into a 9-inch pie plate and flute or crimp the edges. Use other half of dough for a second pie or for top crust on pie.

APPLE PIE

Pastry for pie
1 cup sugar
1 tablespoon flour
½ teaspoon cinnamon

¼ teaspoon nutmeg
4 apples, peeled and
  sliced thin
1 tablespoon butter
¼ cup whipping cream

Make pastry by favorite recipe. Line pie pan with pastry. Mix dry ingredients and sprinkle half of mixture over pastry in pan. Fill pan with thin slices of apples. Sprinkle remainder of dry ingredients over apples. Dot with butter. Pour whipping cream over the whole thing. Put strips of pastry over the top. Bake at 450 degrees for ten minutes. Then reduce heat to 325 degrees and bake for 45 minutes.

APPLE STACK PIE

4 cups applesauce
Pie crust recipe
1/3 cup melted butter
1/3 cup.sugar

1½ teaspoons cinnamon
1½ tablespoons grated lemon
    rind
Whipped cream

Let applesauce chill in refrigerator for several hours. Prepare pie crust and divide the pastry into five equal parts. Roll each part of pastry thin and cut eight inches round, using a plate as a pattern. Place the five rounds on a large cookie sheet. Drizzle with melted butter and sprinkle with mixture of sugar and cinnamon. Chill in refrigerator about five or ten minutes. Bake pastry rounds at 450 degrees until puffy and golden brown. Cool slightly before removing from cookie sheet. Add lemon rind to chilled applesauce. Stack pastry rounds, spreading applesauce generously between each round. Top with whipped cream.

CHERRY-LEMON PIE

1 can sweetened
    condensed milk
1/3 cup fresh lemon juice
¾ teaspoon almond extract

½ cup whipping cream,
    whipped
½ cup chopped almonds
Graham cracker pie crust
1 can cherry pie filling

Mix condensed milk, lemon juice (it must be the freshly squeezed kind), and almond extract together well. Fold the whipped cream into this mixture. Put in refrigerator to chill for about 3 hours. Sprinkle almonds over graham cracker pie crust. Pour chilled lemon mixture over nuts, and pour cherry filling over this. Put in refrigerator until ready to serve.

DATE PIE

14 thin crackers
15 dates

½ cup chopped nuts
1 cup sugar
3 egg whites

Roll crackers fine. Chop dates and nuts into very small pieces. Add sugar and mix well with crumbs. Beat egg whites stiff but not dry and fold them into first mixture. Pour into well-buttered pie pan and bake at 325 degrees about half an hour.

SOUR CREAM PEACH PIE

2 tablespoons flour
¾ cup sugar
2 cups fresh peaches,
  peeled and chopped

1 cup sour cream
1 beaten egg
¼ teaspoon almond extract
½ teaspoon vanilla extract
Pinch salt

Sift flour and sugar together and sprinkle over peaches. Mix. Combine all ingredients and spoon into a pastry-lined pie pan. Bake at 350 degrees about 30 minutes or until filling is set. Then sprinkle with topping made of:

¼ cup butter
1/3 cup brown sugar
½ teaspoon nutmeg

¼ teaspoon ground cloves
¼ teaspoon cinnamon
1/3 cup flour

Cream butter and sugar together. Add other ingredients, mix well, and scatter over top of pie. Return to oven and cook 10 minutes longer.

FRESH COCONUT PIE

2 cups sugar
6 whole eggs
1 cup milk
1 tablespoon melted butter
1 cup grated coconut
Pinch salt

Unbaked 9-inch pie
  shell
4 egg whites, beaten
  stiff
½ cup sugar
½ teaspoon baking powder

Beat sugar and eggs together until fluffy. Stir in milk and butter. Mix well. Stir in ¾ cup of coconut and pinch of salt. Pour into pie shell and bake 30 minutes at 350 degrees. Make meringue of 4 egg whites, beaten stiff, ½ cup sugar, and ½ teaspoon baking powder. Spread on pie, sprinkle with remaining coconut, and bake at 300 degrees for 15 minutes.

MUSCADINE PIE

1 quart muscadines
1 cup sugar
2 tablespoons lemon juice
2 tablespoons flour

Pinch salt
1 unbaked pastry shell
2 tablespoons melted
  butter
Sugar

Pop the pulp out of the muscadines by squeezing between fingers one at a time. Boil the hulls in water to cover until they're tender, about half an hour. Cook the pulp in sugar for about 15 minutes. Then press pulp through a colander or coarse sieve to remove seeds. Drain hulls and add to pulp. Combine lemon juice, flour, and salt and add to pulp and hulls. Pour into pastry shell. Cover with strips of pastry and bake 10 minutes at 425 degrees followed by a reduction of the oven heat to 325 degrees until crust is brown. Brush top with melted butter and sprinkle with sugar before serving.

FANCY STRAWBERRY PIE

3 egg whites
1 cup sugar
1 10-ounce package frozen
  strawberries, thawed

1 tablespoon lemon juice
Pinch salt
½ pint whipping cream
1 baked pie shell
Fresh berries (optional)

Beat egg whites until they form stiff peaks. Then add sugar, berries, lemon juice, and salt and beat for 15 minutes on high speed in electric mixer. Whip cream and fold it in. Spoon into cooled pie crust. Chill in refrigerator at least half an hour before serving. Garnish with fresh berries, if possible.

PECAN PIE

¼ cup butter or margarine
1 cup brown sugar
1 cup dark corn syrup
3 eggs

1 teaspoon vanilla
1 cup chopped pecans
1 unbaked pie shell

Cream butter and sugar well. Add syrup and continue to cream. Add eggs, beating until light and airy. Stir in vanilla and nuts. Pour into unbaked pie crust and bake at 350 degrees for about 50 minutes.

SOUR CREAM PECAN PIE

1 cup sugar
1 cup sour cream
¼ cup sifted flour
¼ teaspoon lemon extract
Pinch salt

2 eggs, separated
Baked pie shell
1 cup brown sugar
1 cup chopped pecans

Add sugar, sour cream, flour, lemon extract, and salt to beaten egg yolks and cook in top of double boiler until thick, about 20 minutes. Cool. Pour into baked pie shell. Beat egg whites until frothy, add brown sugar gradually, and continue beating until light and fluffy. Fold in pecans. Spread over pie and bake at 325 degrees until done, about 15 minutes.

SHAGGY PECAN PIE

3 well-beaten eggs
1 cup sugar
¼ cup melted butter
1 cup milk
3 tablespoons flour
1½ teaspoons vanilla
   flavoring

¼ cup syrup
½ cup pecans
1/3 cup rolled oats
   (uncooked)
1/3 cup coconut
1 unbaked pie shell

Mix everything except the pecans, oatmeal, and coconut. Beat well. Fold in remaining three ingredients and pour into unbaked pie shell. Bake at 350 degrees about 45 minutes or until done.

PECAN BITES

2 3-ounce packages cream
   cheese, softened
2 cups sifted flour
1 cup margarine,
   softened
3 eggs

2 cups brown sugar
3 tablespoons margarine,
   softened
¼ teaspoon salt
1 teaspoon vanilla
1½ cups chopped pecans

Make pastry cups by mixing cream cheese, flour, and margarine and pressing into tart pans or tiny muffin rings, preferably the non-stick kind. Make filling by creaming eggs and sugar, beating in margarine until fluffy and then putting in salt and vanilla. Fill pastry cups about half full of chopped pecans, pour on the filling, and bake at 350 degrees for about 20 minutes.

CHOCOLATE PECAN PIE

2 squares unsweetened
  chocolate
3 tablespoons butter
1 cup sugar
1 cup light corn syrup
3 slightly beaten eggs

1 teaspoon vanilla
Pinch salt
1 cup pecans, coarsely
  chopped
1 unbaked 9-inch pie shell
1 cup cream, whipped

Put chocolate squares and butter in top of double boiler over boiling water until melted. Mix sugar and syrup in pan, and boil for two minutes. Stir in melted chocolate mixture. Pour slowly over eggs, stirring without ceasing. Stir in vanilla, salt, and pecans. Pour into pie shell and bake at 375 degrees about 45 or 50 minutes or until whole top is puffy. Cool. Serve with generous toppings of whipped cream.

CHOCOLATE CHESS PIE

2 cups sugar
½ cup cocoa
1 cup melted margarine

4 beaten eggs
1/3 cup evaporated milk
1 teaspoon vanilla
2 unbaked 9-inch pie shells

Add sugar and cocoa to melted margarine, mixing well. Stir in eggs, milk, and vanilla. When thoroughly mixed, pour into two pie shells and bake at 350 degrees about 35 or 40 minutes. Whipped cream may be added at serving time, but this garnish is entirely unnecessary.

STEAMBOAT BLACK-BOTTOM PIE

14 gingersnaps
5 tablespoons melted butter
4 beaten egg yolks
2 cups milk, scalded
½ cup sugar

1½ tablespoons cornstarch
1½ squares bitter
   chocolate, cut up
1½ teaspoons vanilla
   flavoring
More later

Crumble gingersnaps fine (roll them with a rolling pin), mix with melted butter, and press into a 9-inch pie pan. Bake in 350 degree oven for ten minutes. Cool. Beat egg yolks and add slowly to scalded milk. Put in top of double boiler and stir in sugar and cornstarch. Cook, stirring right often, about 20 minutes or until mixture coats silver spoon. Remove from heat. Pour one cupful of hot custard into small bowl and put the rest of the custard aside for later use. Add the bitter chocolate to the cup of hot custard and beat until smooth and cool. Stir in vanilla. Pour this into the pie crust. Put in refrigerator.

Now for the second layer, assemble:

1 tablespoon plain gelatin
2 tablespoons cold water
4 egg whites
2/3 cup sugar
¼ teaspoon cream of
   tartar

3 tablespoons bourbon
1 cup whipping cream,
   whipped
½ square bitter chocolate,
   shaved

Soften gelatin in cold water and dissolve it in custard set aside earlier (see above). Cool. Make stiff meringue of egg whites, sugar, and cream of tartar. Slowly add bourbon to meringue and fold into the custard. Spread this over the chocolate mixture in the pie. Chill for several hours. Swirl whipped cream over the top of the pie and sprinkle shavings of bitter chocolate over the whipped cream.

CHOCOLATE CREAM PIE

1/3 cup flour
1 cup sugar
2 cups milk, scalded
2½ squares chocolate,
  melted

3 eggs, separated
1 teaspoon vanilla
Baked pie crust
3 tablespoons sugar

Sift flour and 1 cup sugar together in mixing bowl. Bring milk just to boiling point, add melted chocolate, and pour over dry ingredients. Add egg yolks which have been well beaten. Cook this mixture in top of double boiler until it becomes thick. Stir, of course, while cooking. When cool, add vanilla and pour into baked pie crust. Top with meringue made from remaining egg whites and 3 tablespoons sugar, and bake at 350 degrees until meringue is lightly browned.

BUTTERSCOTCH PIE

¾ cup brown sugar,
  firmly packed
1/3 cup flour
¼ teaspoon salt
2 cups milk

3 eggs, separated
3 teaspoons softened
  butter
1½ teaspoons vanilla
Baked 9-inch pie shell
3 tablespoons sugar

Mix brown sugar, flour, and salt together well in top of double boiler. Slowly add milk. Cook over hot water, stirring all the time, until thick and smooth. Beat egg yolks until thick and lemony. Mix a bit of the hot mixture with egg yolks and return to the top of the double boiler. Cook, with no reprieve from stirring, three minutes more. Add butter and vanilla. Cool a bit and then spoon into cooled baked pie shell. Top with meringue made with egg whites and 3 tablespoons sugar and bake at 350 degrees until beautifully browned.

HOMECOMING LEMON MERINGUE PIE

2/3 cup sifted flour
1¼ cups sugar
¼ teaspoon salt
2 cups hot water
3 eggs, separated
1 tablespoon butter

1/3 cup fresh lemon
  juice
2 teaspoons grated lemon
  rind
Baked 9-inch pastry shell
3 tablespoons sugar

    Sift flour, sugar, and salt together into top of double boiler. Gradually add hot water, stirring constantly. Cook over hot water, stirring all the while, until thick and smooth. Pour thick and smooth mixture into three beaten egg yolks, doing it gradually and stirring during the entire process. Add butter (it will melt), lemon juice, and grated rind. When cool, pour into baked shell. Beat egg whites until stiff, gradually adding 3 tablespoons sugar to make meringue. Spread meringue over pie and bake in moderate oven (350 degrees) until meringue is delicately brown.

LEMON CUSTARD PIE

6 beaten eggs
1½ cups sugar
1 tablespoon grated lemon
  rind

2/3 cup fresh lemon
  juice
1½ cups water
Unbaked 9-inch pie shell
Sprinkling of nutmeg

    Put first five ingredients in large bowl and beat (low speed on electric beater) for five minutes. Pour into pie shell and bake at 425 degrees for 25 minutes. Then lower temperature to 275 degrees and bake for 10 minutes longer. Cool on rack. Sprinkle top with nutmeg.

LEMONY BUTTERMILK PIE

3 egg yolks
1 cup sugar
4 tablespoons flour
1 tablespoon butter
2 cups buttermilk
1 teaspoon lemon extract

1 teaspoon grated lemon
 rind
3 egg whites
3 tablespoons sugar
2 unbaked pie shells

Beat egg yolks and the cup of sugar together well. Rub flour into butter, and then add egg mixture, buttermilk, lemon flavoring and grated rind. Pour into unbaked pie shells. Make meringue of egg whites and remaining sugar and spread on top of pies. Bake at 350 degrees until pie shells are done and meringue is brown.

CHESS PIE

This pie (some cooks substitute lemon juice for the vinegar, and some even add a touch of vanilla flavoring) is a favorite at dinners-on-the-ground and big family gatherings.

4 eggs
1¾ cups sugar
1½ teaspoons vinegar

1 tablespoon cornmeal
½ cup butter or
 margarine, melted
Unbaked 9-inch pie shell

Beat eggs with spoon. Stir in sugar and mix well. Add vinegar, cornmeal, and butter. Pour into unbaked 9-inch pie shell. Bake at 425 degrees for ten minutes and then reduce heat to 300 degrees and continue baking for about an hour or until filling is done.

PLAIN MOLASSES PIE

1 cup brown sugar
½ cup molasses
1½ tablespoons flour
2 tablespoons melted butter

3 beaten eggs
Pinch salt
½ cup black walnuts
  (pecans will do)
9-inch unbaked pie shell

Mix all ingredients together well and pour into 9-inch pie shell. Bake at 450 degrees for ten minutes. Reduce heat to 325 degrees and bake for 25 to 30 minutes.

SPICY EGG PIE

4 teaspoons flour
½ teaspoon cinnamon
1 cup sugar
3 well-beaten eggs
1 cup milk

4 tablespoons butter
1½ teaspoons vanilla
2/3 cup shredded coconut,
  sweetened
½ cup raisins
1 unbaked pie shell

Sift flour, cinnamon, and sugar together and add to well-beaten eggs. Mix well. Put milk and butter in small pan and heat to boiling point. Pour over other ingredients (those already spoken of, that is). Stir in vanilla, coconut, and raisins. Pour into unbaked pie shell and bake at 325 degrees for about 35 minutes or until filling is well set and brown. For a fancier pie, sprinkle additional coconut on top of filling after it is poured into pie shell and before baking.

COUNTRY COUSIN EGG CUSTARD PIE

4 eggs	2 tablespoons butter
¾ cup sugar	1¼ teaspoons vanilla
Pinch salt	Unbaked pie shell
2 cups milk	Nutmeg

Combine eggs, sugar, and salt in bowl, mixing well. Heat milk to boiling point, add butter, and pour over first mixture. Mix. Stir in vanilla. Pour into unbaked pie crust, sprinkle with nutmeg, and bake at 400 degrees for ten minutes. Reduce heat to 300 degrees and cook until filling is firm, about 25 minutes.

SWEET POTATO CUSTARD PIE

2 cups mashed sweet potatoes	Juice 1 lemon
2 cups rich milk	1 teaspoon cinnamon
3 beaten eggs	2 tablespoons melted butter
1 cup brown sugar	Unbaked pie shell

Mix mashed sweet potatoes (*they have been cooked, of course*) with other ingredients and pour into pastry shell. Bake at 350 degrees for 40 minutes.

GRANNY TYPE SWEET POTATO PIE

¼ cup butter or margarine	1½ cups milk
1 cup brown sugar	½ teaspoon salt
2 cups sweet potatoes, cooked	1 teaspoon vanilla
	½ teaspoon cinnamon
2 beaten eggs	1 unbaked pie shell

Cream butter with sugar until fluffy. Add potatoes and eggs and beat until light. Gradually add milk. Then stir in salt, vanilla, and cinnamon. Pour into unbaked pie shell and bake at 400 degrees for about 50 minutes or until crust is brown and filling is set.

PEANUT-SYRUP PIE

1 cup sugar
¾ cup light corn syrup
½ cup melted butter or
   margarine

3 beaten eggs
1 teaspoon vanilla
1 2/3 cups roasted peanuts
1 unbaked 9-inch pie shell

Blend sugar, syrup, butter, eggs, and vanilla together well. Stir in peanuts. Pour into pie shell and bake at 375 degrees for 45 minutes. Dry-roasted peanuts, the kinds sold in stores, can be used in this recipe if nobody in the family has time to roast or parch whole peanuts to make the pie.

DEPLORABLY RICH COFFEE ICE CREAM PIE

1 quart coffee-flavored
   ice cream, softened
1 9-inch graham cracker
   pie shell

1 16-ounce can ready-to-use
   fudge frosting
2/3 cup pecan halves

Spread softened ice cream in pie shell. Freeze until firm. Spread frosting over ice cream. Garnish with pecan halves. Freeze stiff. Thaw slightly before serving.

SUGAR PIE, CORNMEAL STYLE

½ cup butter
1 cup sugar
3 eggs
½ cup yellow cornmeal

3 tablespoons fresh lemon
   juice
2 teaspoons grated lemon
   rind
1 unbaked 9-inch pastry shell

Cream butter and sugar well. Beat in eggs, one at a time. Stir in cornmeal, lemon juice and rind. Put in pastry shell and bake at 400 degrees for ten minutes. Lower heat to 325 degrees and bake 15 minutes more, until pie filling is set but not firm. Cool before serving.

PLAIN FRIED PIES

Pastry for 2-crust pie

1½ cups dried fruit, cooked and sweetened to taste

Dried apples, apricots, or peaches are fine for making these old-timey fried pies. Roll the pastry (use standard recipe) about 1/8 inch thick and cut it in circles about 5 inches in diameter. Place on each circle about 2 tablespoons of fruit. Fold the pastry over the fruit and press the edges together well to seal. The tines of a fork help to do this well. Prick the tops in several places. Have a container of deep, hot (375 degrees) fat waiting. Fry the pies, two or three at a time, for about 3 minutes or until brown. Drain well on paper and sprinkle, while hot, with confectioners' sugar.

HOMECOMING GREEN TOMATO PIE

1 pound green tomatoes
4 lemon slices
¾ cup water

1¾ cups sugar
Small piece of ginger
1 unbaked pie shell

Wash and peel firm, green tomatoes and slice them about a quarter of an inch thick. Let slices soak overnight in lime water. Next morning, rinse thoroughly in cold water. Boil lemon slices in the ¾ cup water for 12 minutes. Remove lemon. Stir sugar into water and bring to boil. Add tomatoes, ginger, and cooked lemon slices. Let boil rapidly until tomato slices are clear and syrup is thick. Skim off foam. Cool. Let stand in syrup for awhile after it has cooled. Pour into unbaked pie shell and bake at 400 degrees until pastry is firm and brown.

Salads And Dressings

SALADS AND DRESSINGS

Lettuce is like conversation: it must be fresh and crisp and so sparkling that you scarcely notice the bitter of it.

—*C. D. Warner (1870)*

Most salads start with lettuce. If they don't actually include lettuce among their ingredients, the salads are traditionally served atop crisp lettuce leaves. Lettuce is basic.

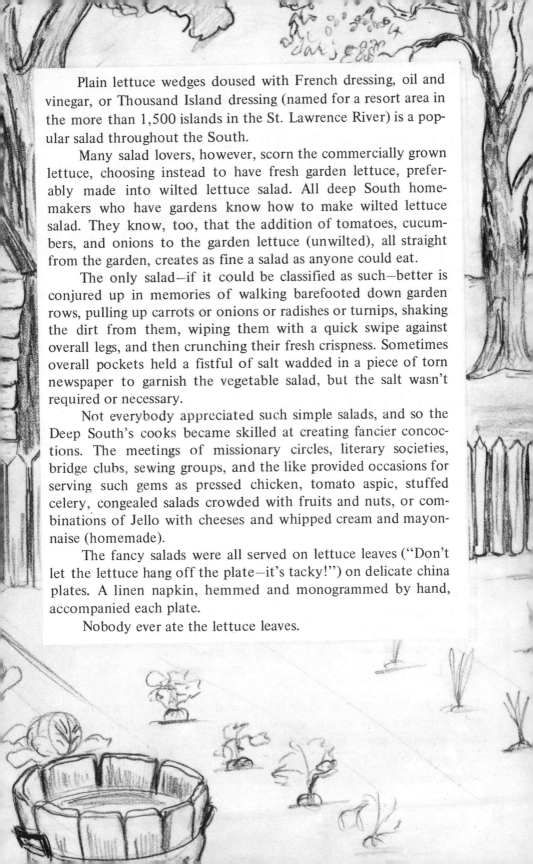

Plain lettuce wedges doused with French dressing, oil and vinegar, or Thousand Island dressing (named for a resort area in the more than 1,500 islands in the St. Lawrence River) is a popular salad throughout the South.

Many salad lovers, however, scorn the commercially grown lettuce, choosing instead to have fresh garden lettuce, preferably made into wilted lettuce salad. All deep South homemakers who have gardens know how to make wilted lettuce salad. They know, too, that the addition of tomatoes, cucumbers, and onions to the garden lettuce (unwilted), all straight from the garden, creates as fine a salad as anyone could eat.

The only salad—if it could be classified as such—better is conjured up in memories of walking barefooted down garden rows, pulling up carrots or onions or radishes or turnips, shaking the dirt from them, wiping them with a quick swipe against overall legs, and then crunching their fresh crispness. Sometimes overall pockets held a fistful of salt wadded in a piece of torn newspaper to garnish the vegetable salad, but the salt wasn't required or necessary.

Not everybody appreciated such simple salads, and so the Deep South's cooks became skilled at creating fancier concoctions. The meetings of missionary circles, literary societies, bridge clubs, sewing groups, and the like provided occasions for serving such gems as pressed chicken, tomato aspic, stuffed celery, congealed salads crowded with fruits and nuts, or combinations of Jello with cheeses and whipped cream and mayonnaise (homemade).

The fancy salads were all served on lettuce leaves ("Don't let the lettuce hang off the plate—it's tacky!") on delicate china plates. A linen napkin, hemmed and monogrammed by hand, accompanied each plate.

Nobody ever ate the lettuce leaves.

WALDORF SALAD

This salad was first served at the original Fifth Avenue Waldorf in New York at a charity benefit in 1893. Oscar Tschirky is credited with being its originator. The 1,500 society leaders who tasted it that night were so delighted with the crunchy salad that its fame spread quickly, and it was not long before hostesses as far away as Alabama were serving it proudly.

1 teaspoon lemon juice
2½ cups diced apples
   (unpeeled)
1 cup celery strips about
   ¾ inch long

¾ cup chopped pecans or
   walnuts
½ cup mayonnaise
Lettuce leaves

Dribble lemon juice over the diced apples. Blend all the ingredients together and serve on crisp lettuce leaves.

FROZEN FRUIT SALAD

2 beaten eggs
1½ tablespoons white vinegar
2 tablespoons sugar
8 large marshmallows

Large can fruit cocktail,
   drained
1 cup thick cream,
   whipped
Lettuce or cabbage

Put eggs, vinegar, and sugar in top of double boiler and cook over hot water (be sure to stir!) until thick. Add marshmallows and stir over the hot water until they melt. Cool. Add fruit and fold in whipped cream. Pour into refrigerator tray and freeze. Cut into squares and serve on lettuce or shredded cabbage.

FRUITED MOLD WITH COCONUT DRESSING

1 can pineapple chunks
2 cups boiling water
2 packages orange gelatin

2 medium bananas, sliced
½ cup chopped pecans
Coconut dressing

Drain pineapple chunks and save syrup. Arrange half of chunks around bottom edge of 2-quart glass bowl. Pour boiling water over gelatin and stir until dissolved. Add enough cold water to pineapple juice to make 2 cups. Add to gelatin mixture. Chill until it begins to set. Fold banana slices and pecans into gelatin, and pour mixture over pineapple chunks in bowl. Chill until firm. Put remaining pineapple chunks in circle around edge of bowl and fill center with Coconut Dressing:

Coconut Dressing

1 cup whipping cream,
  whipped
1 cup grated coconut

½ cup mayonnaise
1 tablespoon confectioners'
  sugar

Mix all ingredients together until blended well.

CRANBERRY-SOUR CREAM SALAD

1 package cherry gelatin
1 cup hot water
1 large can whole
  cranberry sauce

½ cup diced celery
½ cup chopped pecans
1 cup sour cream

Dissolve gelatin in hot water and chill until thick but not firm. Beat cranberry sauce with fork to break up. Stir cranberry sauce, celery, and pecans into gelatin. Fold in sour cream. Pour into one-quart mold and chill until firm.

MARSHMALLOW-LIME SALAD

16 large marshmallows
1 cup milk
1 3-ounce package lime
gelatin
1 3-ounce package cream
cheese

1 large can crushed
pineapple
1/3 cup maraschino cherries,
cut up
1 cup cream, whipped
½ cup chopped pecans

Put marshmallows and milk in top of double boiler. Heat over hot water, stirring every now and then, until marshmallows melt. Dissolve lime gelatin in mixture, stirring well. Chill until mixture begins to thicken. Soften cream cheese and beat until fluffy. Drain pineapple well. Add cream cheese, cherries, and pineapple to marshmallow mixture. Fold in whipped cream and pecans. Chill about three hours before serving.

WHITE SALAD

1 large can sliced pineapple
32 marshmallows
1 envelope plain gelatin
½ cup cold water

¾ cup scalded milk
1 cup cream, whipped
1 cup blanched almonds,
slivered

Using scissors, cut the pineapple slices into small pieces (it might seem easier to use pineapple chunks, but they are too big—rather unladylike). Soak marshmallows and cut-up pineapple in juice from pineapple can overnight. Soften gelatin in cold water and dissolve it in hot milk. Pour into pineapple mixture. Fold in whipped cream and nuts. Pour into mold and chill until firm.

CREAMY RED RASPBERRY SALAD

1 10-ounce package frozen
  raspberries
2 3-ounce packages raspberry
  gelatin
1½ cups boiling water

1 pint vanilla ice
  cream
1 small can frozen
  pink lemonade concentrate
2/3 cup chopped pecans

Thaw berries and drain, saving juice. Dissolve gelatin in boiling water. Add ice cream in small portions, stirring until melted. Stir in thawed lemonade concentrate and raspberry juice. Chill until thick. Fold in berries and pecans. Pour into quart mold and chill until firm.

CRUNCHY SALAD WITH COOKED DRESSING

2 eggs, separated
½ cup milk
½ cup sugar
2 tablespoons cornstarch
3 lemons (juice)

Salt to taste
2 cups tart apples,
  chopped
1 cup chopped celery
2/3 cup white raisins

Beat whites of eggs (not stiff), add yolks, and beat again. Add milk, stirring vigorously. Mix sugar and cornstarch in top of double boiler. Stir in egg-milk combination. Add lemon juice and a dash of salt. Cook over hot water, stirring, until mixture thickens. Cool. Mix apples, celery, and raisins in bowl. Pour cooled dressing over fruit.

CRANBERRIED VEGETABLE SALAD

2 envelopes unflavored
 gelatin
2 cups cranberry juice
 cocktail
1½ cups ginger ale

2 tablespoons tarragon
 vinegar
1 cup shredded cabbage
½ cup grated carrots
½ cup diced green pepper
¼ cup sliced radishes

Soften gelatin in ½ cup cranberry juice. Heat remaining cranberry juice and add gelatin, stirring until dissolved. Add ginger ale and vinegar and chill until mixture begins to set. Fold in raw vegetables. Pour into mold (or individual molds) and chill until firm.

TOMATO ASPIC

4 cups tomato juice
1/3 cup chopped celery
 leaves
1/3 cup chopped onion
1½ tablespoons brown sugar
1 teaspoon salt

2 small bay leaves
3 whole cloves
2 envelopes plain gelatin
3 tablespoons lemon juice
1 cup celery, chopped
 fine

Put two cups tomato juice in boiler with celery leaves, onion, sugar, salt, bay leaves, and cloves. Simmer for four or five minutes. Remove from heat and strain. Soften gelatin in one cup cold tomato juice and add to hot mixture, stirring until dissolved. Add remaining one cup of tomato juice and lemon juice. Put into refrigerator until partially set. Fold in celery. Return to refrigerator until firm.

TOMATO SOUP SALAD

2 envelopes plain gelatin
½ cup water
1 can tomato soup
2 3-ounce packages cream
   cheese, softened

1 tablespoon lemon juice
½ cup diced green pepper
½ cup finely diced celery
¼ cup finely minced onions
½ teaspoon seasoned salt
1 cup mayonnaise

Soften gelatin in water. Heat soup (undiluted) in top of double boiler. Add softened gelatin and stir until dissolved. Remove from heat. Whip softened cream cheese until fluffy. Add to soup mixture, beating until smooth. Cool. Add all other ingredients. Pour into lightly oiled salad mold. Chill in refrigerator until firm.

POTATO SALAD

5 or 6 medium potatoes,
   cubed and cooked
3 hard-boiled eggs, cut
   up coarsely
4 tablespoons sweet pickle
   relish
2 tablespoons green pepper,
   chopped

1 cup diced celery
1 small onion, chopped
½ cup mayonnaise
2 tablespoons prepared
   mustard
Salt and pepper

Combine all ingredients and season to taste. Chill well before serving. Mustard may be mixed with the mayonnaise for easier and smoother addition to the salad. More mayonnaise may be needed—if it is, add it!

221

MELTED CHEESE POTATO SALAD

6 medium potatoes, cooked,
  peeled, and diced
1 cup celery, diced
1 small onion, minced
1/3 cup vinegar
1½ teaspoons seasoned
  salt
¼ teaspoon pepper

2 hard-boiled eggs,
  cut up
½ cup mayonnaise (maybe
  more)
1 tablespoon mustard
2 cups grated sharp
  cheese

Mix all ingredients, except cheese, in a shallow baking dish. Sprinkle cheese on top. Broil until bubbly and golden brown.

STUFFED CELERY

1 cup creamy cottage
  cheese
¼ cup Roquefort cheese
1 teaspoon seasoned
  salt

2 teaspoons whole caraway
  seed
2 dozen 3-inch ribs of
  celery
Minced parsley (optional)

Mix first four ingredients well, and stuff lightly into pieces of celery. Sprinkle with minced fresh parsley, if desired.

WILTED LETTUCE SALAD

2 bunches fresh garden
  lettuce
4 green onions, finely
  chopped

6 slices bacon
¼ cup vinegar
1 teaspoon sugar
¾ teaspoon salt

Wash young lettuce leaves well, drain, and tear into pieces. Put into salad bowl with chopped onions. Fry bacon crisp; drain. In bacon grease in skillet add vinegar, sugar, and salt. Bring to a boil and pour over lettuce. Toss lightly to coat leaves. Crumble bacon on top and serve immediately.

222

CRISP CUCUMBERS IN CREAM

1 large cucumber, sliced
  thin
½ cup vinegar
1/3 cup ice water
1 teaspoon salt

4 whole black peppers
1 medium onion, sliced
  thin
1 cup sour cream
Tomato wedges

Slice cucumber into bowl. Combine vinegar, water, salt, and peppers and pour over. Cover and chill in refrigerator at least 2 hours. Drain well and remove peppers. Mix cucumber and onion slices and toss with sour cream. Serve in small bowls with tomato wedges for color and added taste.

HURRY-UP SAUERKRAUT SALAD

2 3-ounce packages lemon
  gelatin
1¾ cups boiling water
1 tablespoon vinegar
Dozen ice cubes
1½ tablespoons minced
  pimento

6 small green onions,
  chopped
1 large can chopped
  sauerkraut, drained
Lettuce
1 cup mayonnaise
1 teaspoon prepared horseradish

Dissolve gelatin in boiling water. Pour into 9x5x2-inch loaf dish. Add vinegar. Put in ice cubes to hasten setting. Stir constantly until gelatin begins to thicken, about three minutes or so. Remove unmelted ice cubes. Stir in pimento, onions, and drained sauerkraut, stirring with a gentle touch. Chill until mixture is firm. Unmold on crisp lettuce. Mix mayonnaise with horseradish and serve as dressing.

UPTOWN CORNED BEEF AND CABBAGE SALAD

½ cup white vinegar
¼ cup salad oil
¼ teaspoon pepper
½ teaspoon dry mustard
½ teaspoon celery seed
1 teaspoon minced onion
1 teaspoon salt

2 tablespoons sugar
4 cups finely shredded
  cabbage
2 cups cooked corned
  beef strips
1 cup cocktail peanuts
½ cup diced green pepper

Blend first eight ingredients together well. Put cabbage, corned beef, peanuts, and green pepper in large bowl. Add vinegar dressing and toss. Refrigerate covered for several hours. Drain before serving.

LITERARY CLUB PRESSED CHICKEN

1 hen
1 large onion
2 stalks celery (leaves,
  too)
6 hard-boiled eggs
1 small bottle stuffed
  olives
2 envelopes plain gelatin
½ cup cold water

1 cup hot broth (from
  cooking chicken)
6 tablespoons sweet
  pickle relish
1 teaspoon lemon juice
1 teaspoon celery seed
1 teaspoon Worcester-
  shire sauce
Lettuce leaves
Mayonnaise

Put mayonnaise, cream, and sugar in top of double boiler, mix well and heat (do not boil) over hot water. Soften gelatin in ½ cup water. Add to mixture in boiler and blend well. Fold in other ingredients. Pour into mold or bowl, cover and refrigerate until firm. Serve atop lettuce leaves with green pepper rings or stuffed olive slices as garnish.

HIGH COMPANY TURKEY SALAD

8 cups cooked turkey, cut into bite-size pieces
1 large can water chestnuts, diced
1½ cups celery, chopped fine
2/3 cup seedless grapes
1¼ cups slivered almonds

2 cups mayonnaise (may need more)
1½ tablespoons lemon juice
1 tablespoon curry powder
2 tablespoons soy sauce
Lettuce leaves
1 can pineapple chunks

Combine turkey, water chestnuts, celery, grapes, and almonds. Blend mayonnaise with lemon juice, curry powder, and soy sauce. Stir gently into turkey mixture. Chill in large glass bowl for several hours. Serve on crisp lettuce and garnish with pineapple chunks. This salad goes well with a cheese souffle or with hot spoonbread.

TOMATO CUPS FILLED WITH HAM SALAD

6 ripe tomatoes
2 cups cooked ham, diced
½ cup diced celery
1½ tablespoons grated onion
½ teaspoon prepared mustard

2 hard-boiled eggs, diced
3½ tablespoons mayonnaise
1 teaspoon fresh lemon juice
Lettuce

Peel tomatoes and make six cuts in each one, being careful not to cut all the way through. Spread cut sections apart like petals of a flower. Now mix other ingredients together. Fill tomato cups. Serve on lettuce leaves.

HAM AND CABBAGE SALAD

1 cup shredded red
  cabbage
1 cup shredded green
  cabbage
3 stalks celery, diced
2/3 cup cooked ham,
  slivered

½ cup mayonnaise
2 tablespoons prepared
  mustard
Salt and pepper
½ cup pecan halves

Combine first six ingredients in large bowl. Season to taste. Garnish with pecan halves.

FRUIT SLAW

2 sliced bananas
1 cup pineapple tidbits,
  drained

1 cup diced apple (tart)
2 cups shredded cabbage
Coleslaw dressing

Combine fruits and cabbage. Add enough coleslaw dressing (see Confederate Coleslaw recipe) to moisten. Toss lightly. Each serving may be topped with a maraschino cherry.

CARNIVAL CONFETTI COLESLAW

1 small package lime gelatin
1 cup boiling water
½ cup cold water
1 tablespoon vinegar
½ cup mayonnaise

1/3 cup maraschino cherries
  (cut up)
¼ cup raisins
½ cup chopped celery
1 cup grated cabbage
½ cup grated carrots

Dissolve gelatin in boiling water. Add cold water and vinegar. Gradually combine with mayonnaise, mixing well. Chill until it begins to thicken. Fold in other ingredients. Pour into one-quart mold and chill until firm.

CONFEDERATE COLESLAW

1 head cabbage
1 chopped green pepper

1 chopped red pepper
Cooked dressing

Shred cabbage (be sure it is a firm, crisp head) very thin. Mix in peppers and soak in ice water until very crisp. Then drain and pour over it cooked dressing made by mixing 1 teaspoon mustard, 2½ tablespoons sugar, 1 tablespoon flour, and 1½ teaspoons salt and adding to 3 whole eggs, beaten. Stir in 1 cup milk and cook in top of double boiler. Slowly add 1 cup vinegar as mixture cooks. Keep stirring. When mixture starts to get thick, add 1½ tablespoons butter and 1½ teaspoons celery seed. Remove from heat when thick and chill before adding to cabbage-pepper mixture.

MAYONNAISE

This basic dressing was named Mahonnais for Mahon, the main city of Minorca, where the Duc de Richelieu of France got the recipe back in 1628.

1 whole egg
2 tablespoons fresh
   lemon juice

½ teaspoon salt
1 pint salad oil

Beat egg well and add lemon juice and salt. Beat. Continue beating without interruption as oil is slowly, slowly, slowly added. If oil is added too fast or too much at a time, the mayonnaise will separate or curdle. Continue beating a few seconds after the oil is all added. Put in refrigerator to chill. Some cooks add ½ teaspoon dry mustard or 1 teaspoon garlic powder to this recipe. And some, *usually not natives*, add 1 teaspoon sugar.

DRESSING FOR TOSSED SALAD

1 quart real mayonnaise
¼ cup fresh lemon juice
¼ cup vinegar
4 hard-boiled eggs,
  chopped fine

3 cloves garlic, minced
5 green onions, chopped
  fine
3 stalks celery, chopped fine
4 sprigs parsley, chopped

Combine all ingredients well. Put in jars, cover, and keep in refrigerator. Serve over tossed green salad.

CREAM CHEESE-ROQUEFORT DRESSING

1 3-ounce package cream
  cheese, softened
½ cup Roquefort cheese,
  crumbled
½ cup heavy cream

½ cup mayonnaise
1½ tablespoons fresh lemon
  juice
2 teaspoons wine vinegar

Mix cheeses well and beat in heavy cream. Stir in other ingredients. Serve on vegetable salads or on greens.

CELERY SEED DRESSING

½ cup sour cream
2 tablespoons milk
¾ teaspoon celery seed
1 teaspoon dried chives

¼ teaspoon salt
¼ teaspoon coarse black
  pepper
1 tablespoon vinegar

Combine all ingredients except vinegar and mix well. Blend in vinegar. Good with vegetable salads.

COOKED SOUR CREAM DRESSING

2 teaspoons flour
½ teaspoon salt
3 tablespoons sugar
1 teaspoon dry mustard

1/3 cup butter
1½ cups sour cream
2 beaten eggs
1/3 cup wine vinegar

Put flour, salt, and sugar in top of double boiler. Mix. Add mustard and mix well. Put in butter and heat over boiling water until butter melts. Make smooth paste of all ingredients in top of boiler. Add sour cream, eggs, and vinegar. Continue cooking and stirring until mixture is smooth and thick. Cool. Chill before serving. Serve on green salads, egg salads, or vegetable salads.

FRUIT SALAD DRESSING

1 cup mayonnaise
6 ounces cream cheese,
  softened

1 cup thick cream, whipped
1 cup broken nut meats

Beat mayonnaise into cream cheese until well blended. Fold in whipped cream and nuts.

PEANUT BUTTER FRUIT DRESSING

½ cup peanut butter
¼ cup orange marmalade

1 cup orange juice
1 tablespoon lemon juice

Mix all four ingredients together well. Store in covered container in refrigerator. Serve with fruit salad.

MACAROON DRESSING

1 cup sour cream
¼ cup toasted almonds,
  sliced
½ cup flaked coconut

1 tablespoon grated orange
  rind
1½ teaspoons fresh lemon
  juice

Combine all ingredients. Serve over fresh fruit salads. Proportions may be altered to suit individual tastes.

BIT O' HONEY DRESSING

½ cup honey
½ cup salad oil

½ cup lemon juice

Combine these three ingredients. Chill. Serve over fruit salad.

Soups And Sauces

SOUPS AND SAUCES

Only the pure in heart can make a good soup.
—Ludwig von Beethoven, 1817

Along Southern coasts, where the French influence is still strong, instructions for making soup often begin with "First, make a roux."

In other parts of the South, untouched by French ways, soups are made without benefit of a roux.

With or without the roux, a good soup is a pleasant accompaniment to any meal, and a really good soup, thick and rich, is a meal in itself.

Soups may be quickly prepared by opening cans or by adding boiling water to dehydrated mixes, but, though they may temporarily satisfy hunger, such soups lack character. A good soup needs to be personally encouraged to perfection by gentle simmering, frequent stirrings and tastings, random additions of this and that, and even some singing in the kitchen.

Most Southern cooks have no exact recipes for their soups. "You start with a soup bone or seafood or meat of some kind, and you put it in a big pot with fresh water and salt. And after it has simmered on low heat awhile, you add whatever you have on hand—vegetables, potatoes, rice, broth or such—and you let it simmer some more.

"Every time you pass by the stove, you stir the soup and taste it and talk to it a little. Whatever it needs, add it.

"When the flavors all blend, and when their smell lures the family to the kitchen with demands of 'Let's eat! Let's eat right now!' the soup is ready to serve."

On a wintry day (it does get cold in the Deep South), big bowls of steaming soup with wedges of hot corn bread warm the innards and revive the spirits.

And on summer days when the mercury scurries toward 100 degrees, a bowl of cold soup with a crisp salad and a sandwich suffices for lunch or supper.

Soups are economical, and they can be stretched ("Quick—add some water to the soup: there's company coming up the walk!") to

feed unexpected guests, but soups have retained their popularity because, made right, they're good.

One more thing. Recipes for soup may be flexible, but there is one rule: no soup can properly be called gumbo unless it has okra in it. The very word means okra.

Sauces? They're the added touch that transforms bland plainness into gustatory joy. And it is not true that Southerners routinely disguise the taste of everything by covering it with a heavy blanket of catsup. Southerners are more subtle than that!

HUNGRY DAY VEGETABLE SOUP

1 meaty soup bone
8 cups water
1½ teaspoons salt
2 cans tomatoes

1 cup corn
1 cup okra slices
1 cut-up onion
2 cut-up stalks celery
Handful rice (raw, regular)

Put soup bone, water, and salt in big container and simmer until meat on bone is tender and has flavored water in which it is simmering. Add other ingredients. Let simmer several minutes and then taste. Add other seasonings as needed. Do not be limited to vegetables listed above. If there are little dabs of other leftover vegetables in refrigerator, add them during latter part of cooking. Add more water if needed. Stir and taste every now and then. Serve whenever hungry folks ask for a hot bowl of real eating pleasure.

POTATO SOUP

6 medium potatoes,
  diced
1 teaspoon salt
2 slices bacon

1 medium onion, chopped
1/3 cup flour
½ pound ground chuck
1 quart whole milk
Salt and pepper

Cook potatoes in salted water to cover until tender. Mash lightly. Cook bacon until crisp, crumble, and add to potatoes. Saute onion in bacon drippings, and add it to cooked potatoes. Mix flour with ground chuck and brown well in bacon drippings. Add potatoes and mix thoroughly. Stir in milk. Season to taste. Heat to simmering point (not boiling) and serve at once.

ONION SOUP

¼ cup butter
3 large onions, sliced
  thin
2 quarts beef stock, or
  2 cans beef consomme and
  1½ cups water

Salt and pepper to taste
4 slices toasted bread
Grated Parmesan and
  Cheddar cheese

Melt butter in heavy saucepan and simmer onion slices in butter until golden brown. Add the beef stock, or the consomme and water, and seasonings and simmer for about ten minutes. Put a slice of toasted bread (French bread is particularly good—or Italian bread) in the bottom of each soup bowl and cover with steaming soup. When the toast floats to the top, sprinkle generously with the grated cheese. Serve at once.

CREAM OF CABBAGE SOUP

2 cups raw cabbage,
  finely chopped
1 large onion, chopped
4 cups water

1 large can evaporated
  milk
2 tablespoons flour
2 tablespoons butter
Salt and pepper to taste

Cook cabbage and onion in water about 10 or 15 minutes. Add milk to heat. Do not boil. Make a paste of flour and butter, and stir into soup. Cook gently until slightly thickened. Season to taste.

BEAN SOUP

3 cups dried navy
  beans
4½ quarts water
1 meaty ham bone
1½ pounds smoked pork

¾ teaspoon celery salt
1½ tablespoons minced onion
¼ teaspoon dry mustard
Salt and pepper to taste
Parsley (optional)

Cover beans with water and soak overnight. Drain and rinse in clear water. Add water, ham bone, smoked pork, celery salt, and onion. Simmer until beans are very soft. Take out the ham bone and the pork, and dice the meat. Mash the bean mixture through a coarse colander or cream it well by beating it a long time with a wooden spoon. Mix in the meat, mustard, salt, and pepper. Heat to boiling point, stirring all the time. Garnish with parsley if desired.

FRESH GREEN PEA SOUP

1 tablespoon butter
3 cups chicken broth
1 cup potatoes,
  peeled and diced

1 cup fresh green peas
Salt and pepper
1 tablespoon chopped
  parsley

Melt butter in soup pot. Add chicken broth and raw potatoes and simmer until potatoes are soft. Puree mixture in blender. Return to pot. Bring to boil and add green peas. Cook until peas are tender, between five and ten minutes. Season to taste. Stir in chopped parsley.

CREAM OF PEANUT SOUP

2 cups peanut butter
2 quarts milk
2 tablespoons flour

2 tablespoons chopped
  onion
Salt and pepper to taste
Salted nuts (optional)

Thin peanut butter by putting it in a bowl and gradually stirring into it two cups cold milk. Scald the remaining milk in double boiler over hot water and mix it with the flour. Combine with first peanut butter and milk mixture. Add onion, salt, and pepper. Sprinkle salted nuts on top of each bowl of soup, if desired.

CHEDDAR CHEESE SOUP

2 tablespoons butter
1 medium onion, minced
1 carrot, diced
1 stalk celery, diced
2 tablespoons flour

½ teaspoon dry mustard
1 teaspoon salt
1 quart milk
3½ cups sharp Cheddar
   cheese, shredded

Melt butter in heavy pot and saute onion, carrot, and celery until tender. Mash vegetables with fork. Stir in flour, mustard, and salt. Add milk gradually, stirring faithfully. Cook over low heat, stirring still, until thick and smooth. Add cheese, and stir until blended.

CHICKEN SOUP WITH CORN

1 quart chicken broth
1½ cups corn
½ cup celery, chopped
12 pods okra, cut up

Salt and pepper
1 cup cooked chicken,
   cut up
3 teaspoons butter
Additional broth

Heat chicken broth and add corn, celery, and okra. Simmer until vegetables are tender. Season to taste. Stir in chicken and butter. If soup is too thick, add more broth. Simmer for several minutes. Serve with hot wedges of corn bread.

RIVER BOTTOM GUMBO

1 chicken (2-3 pounds),
  cut up
Salt and pepper
Flour
Lard or oil for frying

1 pod red pepper, cut up
1½ quarts okra, sliced
1 large onion, chopped
2 tablespoons flour
1 can tomatoes (sieved)
Hot rice

Season chicken with salt and pepper, roll in flour, and fry brown in lard or oil. Put chicken in heavy kettle and cover with boiling water, adding red pepper. Roll okra and onion in flour, season with salt and pepper, and fry until lightly brown. Put in pot with chicken and add tomatoes. Stir. Simmer for about an hour, adding more water if necessary and stirring often. Serve in shallow soup bowls with a generous mound of hot rice in the center of each bowl.

TURKEY GUMBO

1 turkey carcass, not
  completely bare
3 quarts water
2 onions, diced
3 cups canned tomatoes

4 cups sliced okra
Salt and pepper
3 cups turkey broth
3 cups cooked rice
More turkey, if available

Add turkey carcass to water in large container and simmer, covered, until meat remaining on bones is all cooked off. Remove carcass. Put into the pot the onions, canned tomatoes, okra, and seasonings. Simmer gently for some time. Stir and taste every now and then. Add turkey broth as needed. At serving time, stir in the cooked rice. Heat and serve. Any bits of additional leftover turkey may be added during time soup is cooking.

BRUNSWICK STEW

In pioneer days, this stew always included hunks of rabbit or squirrel. Most cooks agree that beef is no proper ingredient for a real Brunswick stew.

1 hen
2 pounds lean pork,
  cut up
2½ quarts water
2 teaspoons salt
2 teaspoons Worcester-
  shire sauce
Grated rind and juice
  ½ lemon

4 cups whole kernel
  corn
5 large tomatoes,
  cut in hunks
3 potatoes, cut up
2 medium onions, diced
2 cups fresh okra, sliced
2 stalks celery, sliced

Put hen and pork in salted water and simmer in heavy kettle until meat is very tender and is falling off bones. Take the chicken pieces out, remove bones, skin meat, and cut the meat into bite-size pieces. Put the chicken back into the broth, add the other ingredients, and simmer, covered, until mixture is thick. Stir every now and then. Taste occasionally and add salt and other seasonings as needed. Some cooks like to add a cup or two of small green butterbeans to the stew while others say butterbeans spoil the flavor. Other makers of this filling stew recommend the addition of a cupful of blackeyed peas.

OYSTER STEW

4½ tablespoons butter
1 pint select oysters
1 quart milk

1¼ teaspoons salt
Pinch pepper
Paprika

Melt butter in heavy saucepan. Add drained oysters and heat until edges curl. Add milk, salt, and pepper. Heat but do not boil. Sprinkle each serving with paprika.

BARBECUE SAUCE

½ cup chopped onion
4 tablespoons butter
1 cup catsup
½ cup vinegar
2 tablespoons brown sugar
½ cup water

1 tablespoon Worcestershire
sauce
½ large lemon, juice and
rind
Dash Tabasco
Salt and pepper

Saute onion in butter, add other ingredients, and simmer about 30 minutes. Use to baste meat during barbecuing.

SPECTACULAR STEAK SAUCE

1 package dehydrated
onion soup mix
1¼ cups commercial
sour cream

2 ounces blue cheese,
crumbled

Combine all ingredients well. Spread on steaks after they have broiled five minutes. Turn steaks. Broil five minutes, spread with sauce, and serve with remaining sauce.

LEMONY GARLIC BUTTER

1 cup butter, softened
1 clove garlic, crushed
smooth
1 teaspoon seasoned
salt

¼ teaspoon pepper
2 tablespoons fresh lemon
juice
1 teaspoon grated fresh
lemon rind

Cream butter well. Stir in crushed (pureed) garlic, salt, and pepper. Gradually add lemon juice and grated peel. Beat thoroughly. Serve with fish or other seafood.

SEAFOOD COCKTAIL SAUCE

1 cup catsup
2 teaspoons grated
   horseradish (optional)
1 tablespoon grated onion
2 tablespoons vinegar or
   lemon juice

1 teaspoon Worcestershire
   sauce
1 tablespoon pickle
   relish
½ teaspoon salt
Few drops Tabasco

Blend all ingredients well. Put into jar, cover, and chill. Good with raw oysters or boiled shrimp. The horseradish may be omitted.

MUSTARD CREAM SAUCE

2 tablespoons sugar
1½ teaspoons salt
2 teaspoons dry mustard
4 teaspoons flour

2 tablespoons prepared
   mustard
2 eggs
¼ cup cider vinegar
1 cup sour cream

Put dry ingredients in top of double boiler. Add prepared mustard and eggs. Stir with wire whisk or with fork until smooth. Stir in vinegar and sour cream. Cook over simmering water, stirring constantly, until thickened. Cool.

MUSTARD SAUCE

2 beaten eggs
2 tablespoons flour
1 tablespoon dry mustard

1 cup brown sugar
1 cup vinegar
1 cup consomme

Combine all ingredients in top of double boiler. Cook over hot water, stirring all the while, until thick.

CRANBERRY PORT SAUCE

½ cup port wine
3 tablespoons sugar
1 teaspoon ground
  cinnamon

¼ teaspoon ground cloves
Grated rind 1 lemon
1 can whole cranberry
  sauce

Put wine in small saucepan and add dry ingredients to it. Mix well. Simmer over low heat for 5 minutes. Add grated rind and cranberry sauce and beat with fork until mixture is smooth and is well heated. Serve with almost any meat. It is especially good with game and pork.

WILD PLUM SAUCE

Pick ripe plums from roadside thickets. Wash them well, handling gently. Measure them into large, heavy pot, and add 1 cup sugar for each cup of plums. Do not add water: the drops of water that clung to the plums after they were washed will be quite enough. Cook over low heat, stirring occasionally to prevent sticking. When the mixture gets thick, remove it from the fire. Then put it in a colander to remove the seeds and the skins. This sauce is very good with chicken or turkey, and some cooks declare wild duck requires plum sauce to bring out the flavor. This sauce keeps well in the refrigerator for a long time. It may be put into jars and sealed—makes a nice gift.

FRESH LEMON SAUCE

1 cup sugar
2 tablespoons cornstarch
2 cups water
¼ cup butter

2½ tablespoons fresh lemon
  juice
1 tablespoon grated lemon
  rind

Mix sugar and cornstarch in heavy saucepan. Gradually add water. Cook over medium heat until mixture comes to a boil, stirring all the while. Simmer one minute or more to thicken. Stir in butter, lemon juice, and lemon rind.

VANILLA SAUCE

1 cup sugar
2¼ tablespoons cornstarch
Pinch salt

2 cups boiling water
5 tablespoons butter
2 teaspoons vanilla

Mix sugar, cornstarch, and salt in boiler. Gradually add boiling water, stirring as you add. Simmer over low heat, stirring constantly, until thick. This takes maybe five minutes or so. Remove from heat and add butter and vanilla.

FLUFFY RUM HARD SAUCE

½ cup butter
2 cups confectioners'
   sugar
2 tablespoons half-and-half

½ teaspoon vanilla
½ teaspoon rum flavor
1 egg

Cream butter and sugar together well. Gradually add other ingredients and beat until smooth and shiny. Chill in container in which it will be served.

HARD SAUCE

½ cup butter
½ teaspoon vanilla

1 cup confectioners'
   sugar

Combine all ingredients and beat until fluffy. Chill and serve with hot puddings or other desserts.

FRUITED SAUCE

½ cup fresh cranberries
¾ cup sugar
½ cup dried apricots
2 tablespoons flour

1½ tablespoons lemon juice
½ teaspoon grated lemon rind
1½ tablespoons butter

Wash cranberries, cover with water, and add ¼ cup of the sugar. Stir. Cook slowly, stirring as needed, until berries are tender. Meanwhile, cut apricots into small pieces, cover with water, and cook until tender. Drain juice from cranberries and apricots, measure, and add enough hot water to make two cups. Put liquid in heavy saucepan. Add flour and remaining ½ cup of sugar, stirring until smooth. Cook over medium heat, stirring constantly, until mixture is thick and clear. Fold in cranberries, apricots, lemon juice, grated rind, and butter. Heat to boiling. May be served either hot or cold on plain cake, atop pudding, or as a fancy sauce for ice cream.

ORANGY APPLESAUCE

6 cups tart apples
1 orange, juice and grated rind

½ cup sugar

Peel, core, and slice apples thin. Put slices in saucepan with orange juice and grated rind, cover, and cook over low heat until apples are soft. Mash apples to consistency desired. Add sugar, return to heat, and bring to a boil, stirring constantly. Serve hot with meat or use (hot or cold) to embellish gingerbread or plain cake.

LAST-MINUTE ORANGE SAUCE

4½ tablespoons orange juice
1 teaspoon grated orange rind
4½ teaspoons melted butter

¾ cup confectioner's
   sugar, sifted
Bit of salt

Put all ingredients into bowl, and stir vigorously until well blended and smooth. Excellent served over hot nutbread slices.

Vegetables

VEGETABLES

I fight to the finish
'Cause I eat my spinach.

—*Popeye*

It used to be that most Southern vegetables, including spinach, came out of the garden back of the house, and most of those gardens were protected by a scarecrow. Worn-out pants, disreputable sweaters or coats, and battered hats (frazzled sunhats were favored) were saved to "dress the scarecrow in."

Just as the stick man's costume had to be changed annually, so did his position in the garden: crows must not be permitted to become too familiar with either the scarecrow's garments or his location. Familiarity breeds contempt, and a crow with contempt for scarecrows is, to say the least, obnoxious.

The most effective scarecrows had arms made of hickory limbs, according to the dictates of an old Southern superstition.

Not until the scarecrow was in place was the plowing done and the garden made ready for planting. In each community there was a prime plowman, a veteran at plowing up gardens. He and his mule appeared routinely at the homes of his patrons when the warmth of a late winter sun promised the arrival of spring.

Always the plowing was finished before Good Friday, for on Good Friday all potatoes and beans and peas and other vegetables with eyes must be underground. If they're not, they'll cry their eyes out over the Crucifixion. That's why Southern gardens are traditionally planted on Good Friday.

There are other persistent superstitions dealing with the planting and tending and gathering of vegetables.

Corn, for instance, should be planted during the increase of the moon (when the moon is growing from new to full), and six seeds must be planted in each hill to the accompaniment of this rhyme:

One for the cutworm,
Two for the crow,
One for the blackbird,
And two to grow.

It is assumed that the scarecrow in such a garden is now 100-percent effective.

Vegetables that grow underground, such as onions, beets, turnips, carrots, sweet potatoes, etc., should be planted in the dark of the moon, when it is waning.

Hot peppers grow best (and are hottest) if they are planted by a high-tempered redhead. If the services of a high-tempered redhead are not available, the gardener should wait until he himself is very angry before he plants the hot peppers. Otherwise, the peppers will be mild as stale bread.

When the season's first mess of snap beans is picked and snapped, the ends and the strings should be thrown up on top of the house so that the bean vines will grow tall and bear abundantly.

Butterbean hulls should be thrown into the crossroads (preferably a sandy, unpaved crossroad) for the same reason.

And everybody knows that frost must fall on collards before they are fit to eat.

ASPARAGUS ALMONDINE

1 can green asparagus tips
1 can Cheddar cheese
  soup, undiluted
2 hard-boiled eggs, chopped

2/3 cup toasted almonds,
  slivered
1 cup buttered bread crumbs

Mix asparagus, soup, chopped eggs, almonds, and ½ cup of buttered bread crumbs. Place in buttered casserole and spread remaining crumbs over the top. Bake uncovered at 375 degrees about 20 minutes.

FRESH BUTTERBEAN CASSEROLE

4 slices bacon
2 tablespoons bacon
  drippings
1½ tablespoons flour
1 teaspoon salt
¼ teaspoon pepper

2 cups water
3 cups fresh shelled
  butterbeans
2 fresh tomatoes
3 tablespoons grated
  Parmesan cheese

Cook bacon in skillet until crisp. Remove and drain. Pour off all except 2 tablespoons of drippings. Stir flour, salt, and pepper into drippings until smooth. Add water slowly, stirring not slowly, and cook until sauce thickens. Stir in butterbeans. Cover skillet and bake at 350 degrees until beans are tender, about half an hour. Garnish top of dish with sliced tomatoes sprinkled with grated cheese. Crumble bacon on top. Return to oven and bake about five minutes longer or until tomatoes are heated through.

BUTTERY BUTTERBEANS

(Children used to make "cows" out of the speckled beans with the beans for bodies and broom straws for legs, horns, and tail.)

Shell fresh butterbeans, wash and cook gently in simmering water, salted to taste, until beans are tender. During last few minutes of cooking, when water has nearly all boiled away, add about half a cup of rich milk and three or four tablespoons of butter (a tablespoon of butter for each cup of beans), heat well and serve.

Some cooks add several pods of okra to the beans while they are cooking. It is a matter of taste.

BEAN CASSEROLE

1 medium onion, chopped	1 can cream of mushroom soup
2 tablespoons butter	1 can cream of celery soup
2 cans French style green beans	½ cup grated cheese (optional)
1 can bean sprouts	French fried onion rings (optional)

Saute onion in butter. Drain beans and bean sprouts well. Combine all ingredients. Season to taste, pour into buttered casserole, and bake at 325 degrees until bubbly. For extra goodness, add ½ cup grated cheese before baking and garnish with hot French fried onion rings before serving.

SNAP BEANS COOKED WITH HAM BONE

2 pounds fresh snap beans	Salt to taste
1 bone from cooked ham	Small bit of red pepper (maybe)

Wash beans, snap, and string. Put ham bone in large pot, cover with water, and simmer about an hour. Add snap beans and seasonings and continue cooking until beans are tender and meat on ham bone has flavored them properly. Serve with hunks of hot cornbread. Sliced tomatoes are fine with this, too.

COLD NIGHT BAKED BEANS

1 pound dried beans,
  washed well
6 cups water
2 cloves garlic, chopped
1 medium onion, chopped
1 small dried red
  pepper (hot)
½ pound sliced salt
  pork

4 tablespoons molasses
1/3 cup catsup
1 teaspoon dry mustard
1½ teaspoons Worcestershire
  sauce
¾ teaspoon salt
½ cup brown sugar

Put beans in water and bring to a full, rolling boil. Take off stove, cover, and let stand for an hour. Add garlic, onion, pepper, and salt pork and simmer until beans are tender. Dip out two cups of the liquid beans cooked in and drain off the rest. To this liquid add molasses, catsup, mustard, Worcestershire, and salt. Put beans in baking dish, arranging the slices of pork on top. Pour on the liquid. Sprinkle the sugar over the top and bake, uncovered, at 350 degrees about an hour and a half.

FANCY SOUTH GEORGIA CABBAGE

1 medium head cabbage
2 tablespoons melted margarine
¾ cup chopped celery
½ cup chopped green
  peppers

3 cloves garlic, minced
1 cup rich milk
1 cup Cheddar cheese,
  shredded
Seasoning to taste

Cut cabbage into quarters or eighths and cook in a little salted water for about 7 minutes or until tender. Discard water. Chop cabbage fine. Melt margarine in covered saucepan and put celery, pepper, and garlic in pan. Cook over real low heat until vegetables are tender. Mix with chopped cabbage. Now stir in the rich milk (half-

and-half), the shredded cheese, and the salt and pepper as needed. Put into buttered baking dish and bake at 300 degrees for about half an hour. Sprinkle buttered bread crumbs on top during last 15 minutes of baking, if desired.

FRIED CABBAGE

1 firm head cabbage	Salt and pepper
3 or 4 tablespoons bacon drippings	

Wash cabbage and shred. Put in heavy skillet in which bacon drippings have been melted and are hot. Cover and let fry slowly over kinda low heat. Stir occasionally. Season with salt and pepper. Serve with buttered cornbread.

CREAMED CABBAGE

1 medium head cabbage, shredded	½ teaspoon salt
2/3 cup boiling water (salted)	1½ cups milk
	1/3 cup bread crumbs
3½ tablespoons butter	1/3 cup grated cheese,
3 tablespoons flour	if desired

Drop shredded cabbage into boiling water and cook for ten minutes. Drain well and place in buttered casserole. Make cream sauce by melting butter in saucepan, stirring in flour and salt to a smooth paste, and gradually adding milk. Cook, stirring constantly, until mixture thickens. Pour this sauce over the cabbage in the casserole, and cover the top with bread crumbs. Bake at 325 degrees until crumbs are brown, about 15 minutes. Grated cheese may be sprinkled on top of the casserole or mixed in the cream sauce.

DANDY-CANDY CARROTS

1 pound carrots
1 cup orange marmalade

1 teaspoon cornstarch

Wash and scrape carrots and cut into quarter-inch slices. Cook in a little boiling water until tender. Add marmalade (only a dab of water should be left by then) and cook a little longer. Thicken with cornstarch.

BAKED CARROTS

4 cups coarsely grated
   carrots (8 to 10 medium size)
1 tablespoon sugar

1 teaspoon salt
1/8 teaspoon white
   pepper
1/3 cup butter

Butter a small casserole and put the carrots in it. Sprinkle with sugar, salt, and pepper. Toss to mix well. Dot with butter. Cover and bake in 400 degree oven about 25 minutes or until carrots are tender-crisp.

CAULIFLOWER WITH SHRIMP SAUCE

1 large head cauliflower
1 can condensed cream of
   shrimp soup
2/3 cup sour cream

½ teaspoon salt
Dash pepper
½ cup toasted almonds,
   slivered

Cook cauliflower flowerlets in boiling salted water until just tender, about 10 minutes. Remove from water and drain. Put undiluted soup, sour cream, salt, and pepper in saucepan. Mix well. Heat this sauce, but watch (and stir!) carefully so that it does not boil. Place cauliflower in serving dish, pour on the sauce, and top with almonds.

CAIRO, GEORGIA, COLLARDS

Cairo used to boast of being the Collard Capital of the World, but it seems folks do not eat collards often now so the title is used no more. Collards are still good though, and a ham bone or a ham hock or so will turn a pot of collards into a country-style gourmet's delight.

½ pound salt pork   Salt and pepper
1 bunch collards   Hot pepper sauce

Wash salt pork, cut into chunks, and place in a big pot with about six cups of water. Boil gently, covered, for about half an hour. The meat can be boiling while the greens are being washed, picked over, and prepared for cooking. Discard tough outer leaves and stems. Tear washed collard leaves and put in pot with pork. Modern methods stress a short cooking time to preserve vitamins. Older cooks would not think of serving collard greens cooked less than an hour and a half. There is also a difference of opinion as to when to add salt, whether to put it in during the cooking or at the end. Just be sure to add it. Pepper, too, if desired. At serving time, drain the greens and chop coarsely. Put the chunks of salt pork on the platter or in the dish (better) with them. Be sure to have a bottle of hot pepper sauce, preferably homemade, on the table and plenty of cornbread browning in the oven.

FRIED CORN

10 ears fresh corn   1 teaspoon salt
½ cup milk   5 tablespoons butter

Shuck corn, remove silks, and cut kernels from cobs. Scrape cobs gently with back of knife to get juice. Stir milk and salt into corn and pour into heavy skillet in which butter has been melted. Simmer, stirring often, until tender. Add more butter or milk if needed.

CORN FRITTERS

1 cup corn	½ teaspoon baking powder
2 beaten eggs	½ teaspoon salt
½ cup flour	Dash pepper

Combine corn (fresh corn cut from cob is best, but canned corn will do fine) in bowl with beaten eggs. Sift in dry ingredients and beat slightly until smooth. Drop by spoonfuls onto hot, well-greased skillet, turning each fritter to brown well on each side.

CORN-ON-THE-COB

Pull the husks from ears of fresh corn, and carefully pull and brush off silks. Drop in kettle of boiling salted water with water deep enough to cover ears. Cover and cook five minutes. Remove from water. Have plenty of butter and salt waiting. Allow at least two ears for each hungry eater.

The fresh corn may also be roasted in the oven. Pull the husks away from the corn, but do not pull them off. Remove the silks. Pull the husks back over the ears and tie them in place with strips of husks. Soak in cold water for 10 to 15 minutes. Put corn in a baking pan and bake at 350 degrees for 20 to 25 minutes. Remove husks and serve with butter and salt in abundance.

CORN PUDDING

8 tablespoons flour	2 cups whole kernel corn
1 teaspoon salt	4 eggs, beaten until light
5 teaspoons sugar	4 cups rich milk
4½ tablespoons melted butter	

Stir flour, salt, sugar and melted butter into corn. Add eggs to milk and stir in. Pour into shallow, buttered baking pan. Bake at 325 degrees about 45 minutes. Stir pudding from the bottom three times while it is baking.

EGGPLANT CASSEROLE

1 large eggplant
1 small onion, diced
2 stalks celery, diced
1 can cream of mushroom
  soup

½ cup cracker crumbs
½ cup grated cheese
2 beaten eggs
Salt and pepper

'Peel and cut up eggplant. Cook eggplant, onion, and celery in boiling water until tender. Drain well and mash. Add undiluted soup, cracker crumbs, cheese, and eggs. Season to taste and pour into greased casserole dish. Sprinkle a scattering of bread crumbs and a little grated cheese on top and bake at 350 degrees for about half an hour.

FRIED EGGPLANT CIRCLES

Peel eggplant and cut it into rounds (slices) about ¼ inch thick. Sprinkle each slice or circle with salt and pepper to taste. Dip in flour to coat each side well. Fry in butter (just enough to cover the bottom of the pan and to keep circles from sticking—not deep frying!) until brown and crisp. Cook over low heat and turn often to prevent sticking. Some cooks recommend sprinkling each hot circle with sugar just before serving.

EGGPLANT STUFFED WITH OYSTERS

1 large eggplant
½ cup butter
1/3 cup minced onion
1 clove garlic, minced

2 tablespoons minced celery
1 pint oysters, drained
  and chopped
1/3 cup soft bread crumbs
¼ cup minced parsley

Cut eggplant in half lengthwise and scoop out center. Leave wall (peeling or rind) a little more than half an inch thick. Chop eggplant scooped out from center. Melt butter in skillet and saute in it the chopped eggplant, onion, garlic, and celery. Combine remaining ingredients and add to hot mixture in skillet. Fill eggplant shells with mixture. Place shells in buttered baking dish, cover and bake at 375 degrees for half an hour.

LYE HOMINY CASSEROLE, FANCY STYLE

This is fine for taking to covered dish suppers or to dinners-on-the-ground.

3 slices bacon
2 large cans lye hominy
1 cup slivered almonds
1 can cream of mushroom
  soup
2/3 cup coffee cream

1½ teaspoons Worcestershire
  sauce
¼ teaspoon red pepper
  (hot)
1 teaspoon celery seed
½ teaspoon black pepper
1½ cups buttered bread crumbs

Fry bacon crisp and crumble it. Use bacon drippings to grease casserole. Combine (in casserole) lye hominy, bacon, and almonds. Mix soup and cream with seasonings and pour into casserole. Mix gently. Sprinkle bread crumbs on top and bake at 350 degrees for about 35 minutes.

OKRA

1 pound okra
2 cups boiling water
1 teaspoon salt

3 tablespoons butter
Pepper (optional)

Select young, tender pods of okra. Wash well and cut off discolored ends of stems (if they are discolored). Drop into boiling salted water and cook for about 5 minutes. Maybe a little longer. Drain. Put in serving bowl and put butter on the hot pods. Sprinkle with pepper if desired.

SCALLOPED OKRA AND CORN

3 cups sliced okra
4 tablespoons shortening
2 tablespoons flour
1 cup milk
1 teaspoon salt

1/8 teaspoon pepper
¼ pound sharp cheese,
  grated
2 cups canned corn,
  drained
1 cup fine bread crumbs

Fry okra in 2 tablespoons shortening for ten minutes, stirring often. Make cream sauce of 2 tablespoons shortening, flour, and milk. Season. Stir in cheese until melted. Place alternate layers of okra and corn in buttered baking dish. Pour on sauce. Cover with crumbs. Bake at 350 degrees until brown and bubbly.

FRIED OKRA

2 pounds tender okra
¾ teaspoon salt
½ cup cornmeal

½ cup bacon drippings
  or cooking oil

Small pods of okra are usually more tender than larger ones, so choose small pods for frying. Wash and drain well. Slice into rounds, about ¼ inch thick, and discard stem ends and tips. Sprinkle with salt and roll in cornmeal to coat well. Drop into hot fat and cook until golden brown, stirring often.

SWEET AND SOUR ONIONS

4 large onions, sliced
¼ cup cider vinegar
¼ cup butter, melted

1/3 cup boiling water
¼ cup sugar

Grease 1½ quart baking dish. Arrange onion slices in dish. Mix other ingredients and pour over onions. Bake at 300 degrees for about an hour or until onions are tender.

ENGLISH PEA CASSEROLE FOR CHURCH SUPPER

½ cup chopped celery
3 green onions, chopped
¼ cup butter or margarine
1 can condensed cream of
  mushroom soup
1 small can mushrooms

1 small can water
  chestnuts, sliced
1 tablespoon flour
1 large can English peas
½ teaspoon garlic salt
2/3 cup cracker crumbs

Saute celery and onions in butter. Add undiluted soup, mushrooms (save juice), and water chestnuts. Mix flour with liquid from peas and from mushrooms. Stir in first mixture. Add peas and garlic salt. Put in casserole dish, sprinkle crumbs on top, and bake at 350 degrees for 35 minutes.

HOPPING JOHN

1 cup dried black-eyed
  peas
1 medium onion, diced
2 stalks celery, chopped
1 medium ham hock

1 red pepper pod,
  diced
2/3 teaspoon salt
¼ teaspoon pepper
3 cups cooked rice

Cover dried peas with water and soak overnight. Drain and wash in clear water. Drain again. Put peas, onion, celery, ham hock, and seasonings in large container, cover with water, and simmer until peas are tender. Taste to see if more seasonings are needed. Stir in cooked rice and simmer gently a few minutes to combine flavors. Serve in deep bowls. Chunks of ham may garnish each serving.

BLACK-EYED PEAS AND HAM HOCK

2 or 3 small ham hocks
1 pound dried black-eyed
  peas

1 large onion, chopped
Salt and pepper

Cover ham hocks with cold water and cook gently until meat is tender. Remove meat and put aside until cool enough to handle. Then discard bones and skin, and trim off most of the fat. Do not discard the water in which the ham hocks cooked. When this water has gotten cold, skim off the fat that has risen to the top. Now wash the dried peas well and remove all the faulty peas and the little hunks of rock that somehow manage to get mixed in with the peas. Put the washed peas into the water in which the ham hocks were cooked, being sure that it covers them for a depth of one or two inches (add plain water if it does not), and let them soak overnight. Next day, add ham, chopped onion, and salt. Cover kettle and simmer for an hour or so until peas are tender. More water may be needed from time to time. Add seasonings as needed also. While it is not necessary to soak the peas in the water in which the ham hocks were cooked, that water definitely adds to the flavor.

DRIED PEAS WITH TOMATOES AND RICE

1 cup dried peas
2½ quarts water
3 medium onions, sliced

2/3 cup cooked rice
1 cup canned tomatoes
Salt and pepper

Wash peas, pick over them carefully and soak overnight in water. Cook peas in same water until tender. Add onion slices during last half hour or so of cooking. When peas and onions are tender, add rice, tomatoes, salt, and pepper. Pour into buttered 1½-quart casserole, cover, and bake at 350 degrees about half an hour.

STUFFED PEPPERS

6 large green peppers
6 slices bacon
½ pound chopped chicken
   livers
1 cup celery, diced
1 cup onion, chopped

1 clove garlic, crushed
2 cups cooked rice
½ cup mushrooms, sliced
1 teaspoon salt
¼ teaspoon pepper

Wash peppers, cut out stem end, and remove seeds. Put in salted boiling water and cook about five minutes. Drain. Fry bacon in skillet. Remove bacon and use remaining grease (pour off some if there is too much) to cook chicken livers, celery, onion, and garlic. When these are tender, add rice, mushrooms, and seasonings. Mix well. Use mixture to stuff peppers. Put stuffed peppers in baking pan, add ½ inch of water to bottom, cover, and bake at 375 degrees for 25 minutes.

NEW POTATOES AND SNAP BEANS

2 pounds fresh beans
Small ham hock
Water

Salt to taste
1 pound small, new
   potatoes

Snap the ends off the beans, string them, and break them into pieces about two or three inches long. Put ham hock in a large pan with enough water to cover it and cook, covered, for about 20 minutes. Add beans and continue cooking. Meantime, scrape the potatoes and put them on top of the beans, sprinkling them well with salt. Cover the pot and continue cooking until potatoes and beans are tender. Add more water if needed. Taste a bean or two to make sure they are salty enough.

These beans are known by several names: snap beans, green beans, string beans. They are all about the same. All good.

NEW POTATOES, COMPANY STYLE

12 new potatoes (small)
¼ cup butter
¼ cup flour
2 teaspoons salt
Pinch pepper

2 cups milk
1/3 cup chopped onion
¾ cup sliced celery
1½ cups English peas

Scrub potatoes. Boil in salted water until tender. Make cream sauce by melting butter in saucepan, blending in flour and seasonings, and gradually stirring in milk. Cook over low heat, never once letting the stirring cease, until thick. In another saucepan, cook onions and celery until tender. Now put potatoes in serving dish. Add most of the peas and most of the celery-onion mixture (drain all of them well) to the sauce and pour this sauce over the potatoes. Put the remaining vegetables on top of the sauce.

POTATOES AND SAUSAGE

4 big potatoes
1 big onion
Seasonings

1 pound link pork
  sausage
2½ tablespoons cooking oil

Peel and dice potatoes and onion, mix, and season. Cut sausage into small pieces. Put potatoes, onion, and sausage into hot oil in thick skillet and cook over low heat until potatoes and onion are tender. Pour off sausage fat as it accumulates in skillet.

HEARTY BREAKFAST DISH

Peel three medium-sized sweet potatoes and cut them into ¼-inch slices. Slice three medium-sized apples, leaving red peelings on to add color. Place apple and potato slices in hot skillet with 4 tablespoons of melted butter. Sprinkle ½ cup brown sugar on top, and add a sprinkle of salt. Cover and cook over low heat for about half an hour, turning the slices occasionally.

GLAZED SWEET POTATOES AND APPLES

6 sweet potatoes
3 cooking apples, peeled
  and sliced

½ cup butter
2/3 cup brown sugar
1 tablespoon water or
  lemon juice

Scrub potatoes and put them in large container of boiling water. Cook until tender. When cool enough to handle, peel and slice in half-inch slices. Put half the slices in the bottom of a buttered casserole, sprinkle a little brown sugar (about 2 tablespoons) on top, cover with apple slices, and put remaining potatoes on top of apples. Melt butter in small pan. Add remaining sugar and water or lemon juice. Heat until sugar melts and mixture reaches boiling point. Pour over potatoes. Bake at 350 degrees about 50 minutes. Some cooks like to drizzle a little honey over the apple layer and squeeze lemon juice on it. About 1/3 cup apple juice poured over casserole enhances the flavor. There are many possibilities.

SWEET POTATOES AND PECANS IN A SKILLET

1/3 cup butter
1/3 cup pecan halves
1 tablespoon cornstarch
½ cup water
¾ cup light brown
  sugar, packed

1 tablespoon grated orange
  rind
1 cup orange juice
6 to 8 cooked sweet potatoes,
  quartered

Melt butter in heavy skillet and saute pecans in it until nuts are crisp. Stir frequently. Remove pecans, drain, and set aside. Blend cornstarch with water. Stir into butter in skillet, making smooth paste. Slowly add sugar, grated rind, and orange juice. Cook over medium heat, stirring constantly, until sauce boils. Add sweet potatoes and heat thoroughly, spooning the sauce over them as they heat. Serve topped with the crisp pecans. Canned potatoes, well drained, may be used in this recipe also.

TIPSY 'TATERS

1 cup chopped pecans
1 cup grated coconut
3 tablespoons brown sugar
1 cup raisins
2/3 cup peach brandy
4 cups cooked sweet
   potatoes

12 large marshmallows
1 4-ounce bottle
   maraschino cherries
2 tablespoons juice from
   cherries

This is not a spur-of-the-moment dish. The night before it is to be served, mix the pecans, coconut, sugar, raisins, and brandy, stirring well and storing it in a covered dish in the refrigerator. Next day, mash the cooked sweet potatoes and beat until they are fluffy. Stir fruit mixture into the potatoes. Taste. A little more sugar may be needed. Put half of mixture into a buttered casserole (it will take a big size). Put marshmallows on top of this and cover them with the rest of the potatoes. Arrange the cherries (drained) on top and then sprinkle a little cherry juice around the cherries. Bake at 350 degrees for 20 minutes.

CANDIED SWEET POTATOES

4 or 5 large potatoes
1 cup brown sugar

3 tablespoons melted
   butter
3 tablespoons orange juice

Boil potatoes until tender. Drain and peel. Cut into halves or quarters and place in shallow, buttered baking dish, one layer deep. Sprinkle with brown sugar, drizzle with melted butter, and pour orange juice over and around. Bake at 425 degrees about 15 minutes, basting with syrup every now and then.

RUTABAGA SOUFFLE

2 cups rutabaga, cut up
1½ teaspoons sugar
½ pint sour cream
2 tablespoons butter

1 teaspoon baking powder
Salt and pepper
2 eggs, separated
Buttered bread crumbs

Put rutabaga and sugar in saucepan with water, and boil until rutabaga is tender. Drain and mash rutabaga. Mix rutabaga, sour cream, butter, and baking powder, and season to taste. Beat egg yolks and add. Beat egg whites until stiff and fold them into mixture. Spoon into small, buttered baking dish and cover with buttered bread crumbs. Bake at 350 degrees for half an hour.

SPINACH RING

2 cups cooked spinach,
  chopped
1 cup white sauce

3 beaten eggs
½ cup grated sharp cheese
Salt and pepper

Mix all ingredients together well. Pack in buttered mold and put this mold in a pan of hot water with enough water to come up about an inch and a half on the sides of the mold. Bake at 375 degrees for about 50 minutes. At serving time, remove from mold and fill center with buttered carrots or with pickled beets.

BAKED SPINACH

2 cups chopped spinach
1 lightly beaten egg

2 tablespoons vinegar
¼ cup cream
Salt and pepper

Mix all ingredients and place in well-greased, 1½-quart casserole. Bake at 350 degrees until set, about half an hour.

SQUASH SOUFFLE

10 medium squash
1 small onion, chopped
½ teaspoon salt
1 cup grated cheese

½ cup rich milk
2/3 cup cracker crumbs
1½ tablespoons butter,
  melted
2 eggs

Slice squash and cook in salted, boiling water with onion until tender. Drain well. Stir in cheese, milk, and cracker crumbs. Stir in melted butter. Beat eggs well and fold in. Pour into buttered casserole and bake at 350 degrees for about 25 minutes. Part of the grated cheese may be sprinkled on top of the mixture before it is baked, if desired.

COUNTRY SQUASH

8 to 10 yellow squash
1 teaspoon salt
½ cup butter or margarine

1 large onion, chopped
Black pepper

Wash fresh, tender squash, slice thin, and cook in boiling, salted water about ten minutes. Drain. Melt ¼ cup of butter in heavy skillet and slowly cook onion until tender. Add squash. Press down. Add rest of butter and lots of pepper. Cover and cook 30 minutes, stirring often.

FRIED SQUASH BALLS

2 cups cooked squash
1 onion, chopped
2 well-beaten eggs
1 cup soft bread
  crumbs

Salt and pepper
½ cup crushed dry
  crumbs
Hot fat

Drain squash well and stir in onion. Add eggs and bread crumbs. Shape into small balls, salting and peppering each one. If the squash is too moist to shape into balls, add more bread crumbs. Roll in crushed crumbs. Chill balls about 6 hours. Fry in deep, hot fat.

SQUASH AND SPRING ONIONS

Wash tender yellow squash and slice. Layer in buttered baking dish with sprinklings of salt and pepper (some cooks like a smidgen of sugar) and dabs of butter. Cover with a generous layer of chopped green onions. Continue until squash and onions are used up—or dish is full. Cover and bake at 350 degrees about 35 minutes.

SCALLOPED TOMATOES

6 or 7 large, ripe tomatoes
1½ tablespoons grated onion
1 teaspoon sugar

¼ cup melted butter
Seasonings to taste
1½ cups soft bread crumbs

Peel tomatoes, cut them up, and put them in a saucepan. Cook over low, low heat for about 10 minutes. Stir and mash (this gets the juice out) while cooking. Stir in grated onion, sugar, butter, and salt and pepper to taste. Put layer of this mixture in buttered casserole, cover with bread crumbs, and repeat until everything is used up. With proper planning and luck, there will be bread crumbs left to go on top. Bake at 375 degrees about 25 minutes.

LATE CROP FRIED GREEN TOMATOES

4 large firm green tomatoes
½ cup cornmeal or flour
1¼ teaspoons salt

¼ teaspoon pepper
Bacon drippings

Cut tomatoes into slices about a quarter-inch thick. Mix cornmeal (or flour), salt, and pepper together and coat tomato slices with this mixture. Have hot bacon drippings waiting in heavy skillet. Fry slices slowly until brown, turning them once. Drain and serve. These fried green tomatoes are welcome with almost any dish, and they are particularly fine when served with scrambled eggs. Cooking oil may be substituted for the bacon drippings, but it is not quite as good.

TURNIP GREENS WITH CORNMEAL DUMPLINGS

¼ pound salt pork   Salt to taste
1 or 2 bunches of tender,
  fresh turnip greens

Cut the salt pork into hunks or score it deeply. Put it into pot with enough water to cover well. Cover pot and bring to a simmering boil. Add turnip greens which have been thoroughly washed and from which woody or tough stems have been removed. Lower heat, cover, and cook about an hour and a half or two hours. Taste to see how much salt is needed (some salt pork is so salty no extra seasoning has to be added). Do not let the pot boil dry—add water as needed.

Now make the dumplings by mixing together 2 cups cornmeal (water-ground variety, if available), 1 teaspoon salt, 1 tablespoon melted bacon drippings, and about a cup (maybe more) of boiling water. Shape into small pones and place on top of turnip greens in pot. Baste with a little pot likker. Cover pot and simmer for about 20 minutes or until dumplings are done the taste test is the most reliable. Remove from heat and have plenty of homemade pepper sauce ready to serve with this real Southern delicacy.

INDEX

Frostings And Fillings

Candy

Cheese and Eggs

Meats, Game, Poultry and Fish

Meats

Game

Poultry

Salads And Dressings

Soups And Sauces

Vegetables

274